Reconciliation: The Sacramental Path to Peace

David E. Rosage

LIVING FLAME PRESS

BOX 74 LOCUST VALLEY, N.Y. 11560

All Scripture quotations are taken from the *New American Bible.*

Nihil Obstat: Rev. Armand M. Nigro, S.J.

Imprimatur: Most Rev. Lawrence H. Welsh, D.D.
              Bishop of Spokane

Cover: Robert Manning

Copyright © 1984 by David E. Rosage

Published by: Living Flame Press/Locust Valley/New York 11560

Publication date:
Feast of the Triumph of the Cross
September 14, 1984

ISBN: 0-914544-56-X

Printed in the United States of America.

*To all priests who minister
the healing, forgiving love
of the Lord through the
Sacrament of Penance*

Table of Contents

Introduction

WHAT HAPPENED TO SIN?

In the afternoon or evening of life one may well look back rather nostalgically and wonder why the Sacrament of Penance is not more fully appreciated and used more frequently. On the other hand, younger persons not yet in the habit of receiving the Sacrament of Penance regularly may regard the Sacrament with its personalized and formal absolution unnecessary and irrelevant: "God will forgive me; I have no need of any other channel of forgiveness."

Sense of Sin

Many reasons are alleged for indifference to the Sacrament of Reconciliation. Perhaps the most important is that we have lost our sense of sin. The world does not accept the concept nor the reality of sin. Consequently we are deprived of the consolation of God's mercy, compassion, forgiveness and healing flowing from his infinite love. Pope Pius XII emphatically alerted us that the world was losing its sense of sin. Since that time the sense of sin has been continuously fading even though the Church continues to warn us of this.

Conscience

We are asked to accept more responsibility for forming our own conscience. Rules and regulations have been gradually withdrawn. The Church did so with the hope that our response would be a loving service rather than a conduct imposed by legalistic requirements.

In this time of transition, the pendulum has swung to the opposite extreme. Hopefully it will swing back into a more centered position. St. Thomas reminds us that virtue usually stands in the middle course.

Today we seem to be able to excuse sin of every kind. We use such excuses as "God understands," or "God would never expect this of me under these circumstances," etc. Such excuses rest very much on feelings rather than on objective principles of morality.

Some psychologists have done their share to convince us that certain modes of action are psychological needs and not morally wrong. They would have us believe that certain behavior once considered immoral is necessary and essential for the maturation and emotional health of our human personality.

Healing

Another reason why the Sacrament of Reconciliation has fallen into disuse is the fact that we have forgotten the need we have for healing. Have we concentrated so very much on an exact and detailed examination of conscience, the correct recital of our sinfulness and our need for forgiveness that we have forgotten our need for healing? Sometimes we need healing more than forgiveness. What we may regard as a sin may be only the symptom of something within us which requires healing.

How often should we receive the Sacrament of Reconciliation? As often as we need healing. Is there anyone who does not recognize his or her need for continual healing?

Examen

In the past some have plagued themselves in preparing for the Sacrament of Penance with a laborious and exacting examination of conscience, and then recited a detailed account of all their faults and failings. This can cause anxiety and a fear of forgetting something. This also contributes to making the Sacrament distasteful.

Universal Redemption

Each time we receive this Sacrament we encounter the risen, glorified Jesus, who waits to greet us with all his forgiving, healing, redeeming love.

By his passion and death on the cross, Jesus redeemed the whole human race — everyone who would ever live. A marvelous truth! Yet we may suffer anxiety about our own personal forgiveness and the application of his redemption to us personally. "Did Jesus really forgive this particular sin of mine?"

In keeping with today's emphasis on personhood, we seek to know personally and individually that we are forgiven and healed. In the Sacrament of Penance, Jesus personalizes his forgiveness as we encounter him in this mystery of his mercy and compassion.

Jesus' Role

Jesus suffered and died for our sins. He is now in his glory at the right hand of the Father. But what is his glory? His continuing role as Savior and Redeemer of us. Each time we meet him with the proper dispositions in this Sacrament, we are saying, "Jesus, I need you as my Savior," and all of us need to be needed. Jesus is no exception. "I am open to whatever transformation you wish to effect in me." This gladdens the heart of Jesus.

Attitudinal Adjustment

We need a change of attitude. The reflections in these pages draw our attention to only one aspect of the problem — our loss of a sense of sin.

It will be fruitful and also facilitate our coming to a better appreciation of the Sacrament of God's loving mercy and forgiveness, to relive with Jesus some of the episodes in the Gospel where he confronts sinners and reaches out to them in loving forgiveness and healing. This book offers us a glimpse into some of these episodes.

Jesus said:

"I am the light of the world. No follower of mine shall ever walk in darkness; no, he shall possess the light of life" *(John 8:12)*.

The closer we come to a bright light the better we see. As we approach Jesus, the light of the world, our vision and understanding become clearer. Jesus points out to us the malice of sin.

He helps us to understand that sin is saying "no" to love. Sin is tragically refusing to love. Sin is rejecting the love of Jesus.

HOW TO USE THIS BOOK

This is not so much a book of information and instruction as a compendium of scriptural reflections for meditation and contemplation. We are invited to read between the lines and listen to what the Lord is saying to us.

As we meet Jesus in his Word, our own faults and failures, our infidelities and sinfulness, become more evident; but more important we become more deeply aware of his all-embracing love forgiving, healing and redeeming us at every turn.

As we listen, the Word of the Lord should find a home

in our hearts. Listening is simply being for God and letting God be for us. It is resting in his presence. We activists need to learn to linger with the Lord, to listen to what he is trying to say. Even if nothing seems to happen within us, his Word molds and transforms our attitudes and hearts.

As we eat at the table of the Lord's Word, his Word nourishes and strengthens, inspires and motivates us. Drawing closer to Jesus, the light of the world, we see more clearly those obstructions and barriers which hinder him from investing us more fully with his divine life and love.

Jesus pointed out the true greatness of his Mother as a hearer of the Word. A woman in the crowd praised Mary because she had given birth to Jesus. Jesus, though pleased with this compliment, pointed out Mary's real greatness.

"Rather . . . blest are they who hear the word of God and keep it" (Luke 11:28).

Power-Packed Word

The Father speaks through Isaiah:

"For just as from the heavens the rain and snow come down and do not return there till they have watered the earth, making it fertile and fruitful . . . So shall my word be that goes forth from my mouth; It shall not return to me void, but shall do my will, achieving the end for which I sent it" (Isaiah 55:10-11).

His Word will achieve the end for which he sent it, if we permit it to do so. The all-important condition is to spend time in the prayer of listening, being open and receptive, totally for him and letting him be fully for us.

His Word sinks into our hearts and transforms us. It changes our attitudes. Prayer time is an attitudinal adjustment hour.

Though our hearts are being transformed we may not

11

be intellectually aware of what is happening. The Lord simply asks us to trust him.

Gift of Self

Our problem is to be sufficiently generous to give that time graciously to the Lord. It means a readjusting of priorities, a dying to self by detaching ourselves from less important preoccupations.

Are we willing to accept the Lord's invitation: "Come by yourselves and rest a little" *(Mark 6:31)?*

Format

Each chapter is intended for a day's prayer and reflection. The Scripture passage should be read slowly and reflectively, letting each word find a home in our hearts. If a certain word, phrase or expression strikes a resonant chord within us, we should rest and linger with it and not hasten to finish the rest of the passage.

Reflection

The commentary which follows the Scripture passage in each chapter is intended to activate our imaginations, to give us new or different insights and to energize our meditation and lead us into contemplation.

Review of Life

The Review of Life is basically an examination of conscience. Its purpose is to help us survey honestly and objectively our attitudes and actions, to discover where we may have been remiss. There may be areas of our lives which we will wish to ponder other than those mentioned in the questions proposed.

Colloquy

A colloquy is a relaxed conversation of one friend with another concerning mutual interests, seeking information or advice, sharing an experience or expressing gratitude and appreciation. Our prayer time should always end with a colloquy with our loving Father, with Jesus and with the Holy Spirit. It can also be addressed to our heavenly Mother or any of our favorite saints. The colloquy capsulizes our reflections and pinpoints the particular grace we are seeking.

If these pages help us recognize some fault or failure impeding the transformation our Lord is trying to effect within us, we lift our hearts in praise and thanksgiving to our compassionate Father.

Hopefully these reflections on our waywardness will cause genuine joy not only in our own hearts, but even in heaven:

"There will likewise be more joy in heaven over one repentant sinner than over ninety-nine righteous people who have no need to repent" *(Luke 15:7)*.

Let us ask Mary, the sinless one, to: "Pray for us sinners now and at the hour of our death."

The Father's Love

1

Collision Course

"Yes, God so loved the world that he gave his only Son, that whoever believes in him may not die but may have eternal life. God did not send the Son into the world to condemn the world, but that the world might be saved through him" *(John 3:16-17)*.

According to God's original plan, our first parents were destined to be eternally united with him in perfect bliss, provided they proved themselves by remaining faithful to God's wishes. Unfortunately, they refused the love which God held out to them. They wanted more — they wanted to be like God himself.

By their willful act, they severed their personal relationship with the Lord God, who could not tolerate this rebellion. He could have utterly destroyed them, but he is a God of mercy and compassion.

Since sin severed Adam and Eve's union with God, they could no longer live in the Garden:

"The Lord God therefore banished him from the garden of Eden, to till the ground from which he had been taken" *(Genesis 3:23)*.

That same rebellion continues in our hearts. We play God. We want to be a law unto ourselves. We want to be our own interpreter of the law, especially in matters of moral conduct.

In his great compassion, God promised our first

parents, and us, a Redeemer who would eventually reestablish this ruptured relationship. In this process of redemption, we would once again have the capacity to receive God's divine life and love. God promised:

"I will put enmity between you and the woman, and between your offspring and hers; He will strike at your head, while you strike at his heel" *(Genesis 3:15)*.

God is faithful. Throughout the Old Testament, God reiterated, clarified and renewed that promise over and over again. The Chosen People turned away from God on so many occasions to the worship of false gods, but God remained faithful to his promises and never abandoned them.

In order to bring them back, he permitted them to be led into exile, war, pestilence and famine until they came to their senses again. God is not vengeful or vindictive, but he used these means to bring his people back to him.

How often in the Scriptures we hear God say:

"I will be your God and you shall be my people."

In the fullness of time, God fulfilled his promise.

"Yes, God so loved the world that he gave his only Son, that whoever believes in him may not die but may have eternal life" *(John 3:16)*.

St. John writes:

"God's love was revealed in our midst in this way: he sent his only Son to the world that we might have life through him" *(I John 4:9)*.

Our broken, sinful human nature needs redemption. An infinite chasm exists between unredeemed people and God. Of ourselves alone we are not capable of receiving the gift of his divine life.

In Baptism, Jesus offers us the fruits of his redemption,

17

uniting our human nature with the divine life. We become the adopted sons and daughters of his Father. We are the temples of the Holy Spirit. This is our true dignity.

''''You are the temple of the living God, just as God said: 'I will dwell with them and walk among them. I will be their God and they shall be my people. . . . I will welcome you and be a father to you and you will be my sons and daughters' '' (II Corinthians 6:16ff).

REVIEW OF LIFE

Am I aware of my real dignity as an adopted son or daughter of my loving Father?

Do I question God's providence — mistrust him — doubt him?

Do I play God by judging others, criticizing them not knowing the real motives for their actions?

Do I try to exempt myself from God's law in order to do something I want to do?

PRAYER

Father, how wonderful your care for us! How boundless your merciful love! To ransom a slave you gave away your Son. O happy fault, O necessary sin of Adam, which gained for us so great a Redeemer!

— Easter Vigil

2

A Forgiving Father

"It is I, I, who wipe out, for my own sake, your offenses; your sins I remember no more" *(Isaiah 43:25).*

Some think of the God of the Old Testament as a severe God, who is eager and anxious to punish every infraction of the law. Some see him as a God who retaliates and delights in taking vengeance on his people.

God did permit his people to be defeated in war, to be led into captivity, to be exiled, to suffer famine, but these were only means by which he could bring his stiff-necked people back to realize that he and he alone was their God, and he alone was their salvation.

In Sacred Scripture God our Father reveals very much about himself. Speaking to us through the prophet Isaiah, he says:

"It is I, I, who wipe out, for my own sake, your offenses; your sins I remember no more."

If sin is a rejection of God's love, how could God say that he is wiping out our sins for his own sake?

There is mystery here. God is eternal mystery. We can never fully understand the immensity of God's love.

However, God's overwhelming love radiates through this mystery. His love is an infinite, immutable, enduring, eternal love.

One of love's characteristics is that it must give. It must

be translated into action to please the beloved. This is true especially if the lover is the only person who can do a certain thing for the beloved. If this is true of human love with all its self-centeredness, how much truer is it of divine love.

Only God can forgive sins. God's creative love brought us into existence. His providing love sustains us at every moment of our earthly sojourn. His forgiving, healing love is always ready to remove any obstacles which threaten our union with him.

We cannot earn or merit God's love. There is only one condition necessary for us. We must be open and receptive to accept it. We must honestly want to be forgiven. This disposition is absolutely indispensable.

God respects our free will. He does not impose his healing, forgiving love upon us. Of ourselves we cannot wipe away or atone for our own sins, but we can humbly acknowledge our sinfulness and our need for his forgiveness.

We must be sorry for our sinfulness. Sorrow is the fruit of love. When we realize God's overwhelming love for us in spite of our past refusal to accept his love, how can we help but respond in love?

If we truly love God, we will want to do what pleases our loving Father. As Jesus said:

"He who obeys the commandments he has from me is the man who loves me" (John 14:21).

And again:

"Anyone who loves me will be true to my word, and my Father will love him; we will come to him and make our dwelling place with him" (John 14:23).

If we love, we will not look upon the commandments as rules and regulations restricting our liberty, but as ways and means of doing something to please our gracious Father.

Jesus was always concerned about doing the Father's will perfectly. This was His love-offering to the Father.

The Father knows the dispositions of our hearts. When he sees that we are striving to love him, he assures us:

> "It is I, I, who wipe out, for my own sake, your offenses; your sins I remember no more."

REVIEW OF LIFE

Do I recognize and appreciate God's compassion as revealed through the prophets in the Old Testament?

Do I respond generously and trustingly to his forgiving, healing love?

Do I believe strongly enough that God really wants to forgive me more than I could want it myself?

Do I pause frequently to ask God to have mercy on me, a sinner?

COLLOQUY

Father, what comfort and consolation your reassuring words bring me: "Your sins I remember no more." The burning fervor of your love consumes the wretchedness of all my sins. I cannot understand nor comprehend such love, but my heart cries out: Thank you for loving me and I love you, too.

3

Heart Transplant

"I will sprinkle clean water upon you to cleanse
you from all your impurities, and from all your
idols I will cleanse you. I will give you a new heart
and place a new spirit within you, taking from your
bodies your stony hearts and giving you natural
hearts. I will put my spirit within you and make
you live by my statutes, careful to observe my
decrees. You shall live in the land I gave your
fathers; you shall be my people, and I will be your
God" *(Ezekiel 36:25ff)*.

The prophet Ezekiel portrays God as a caring, concerned, forgiving Father. Despite Israel's many defections,
God was always eager to take them back as his own people
whenever they showed signs of repentance.

God's attitude has never changed. He treats us in the
same way. If we fall into sin, he is willing and anxious to
take us back, to forgive and to heal:

"I will sprinkle clean water upon you to cleanse
you from all your impurities, and from all your
idols I will cleanse you."

Water, a cleansing agent, is the symbol of purification.
We use holy water at entrances of our churches and
chapels to remind us to cleanse our hearts as we enter to
pray.

At Mass, after the preparation of the gifts, the priest

cleanses his hands and prays: "Lord, wash away my iniquity, cleanse me from all my sins."

The Lord continues his redeeming process by transforming our hearts, by detaching us from those things which wean us away from him. How does he accomplish this?

"I will give you a new heart and place a new spirit within you, taking from your bodies your stony hearts and giving you natural hearts."

This "new heart" and "new spirit" effects a whole conversion process within us and helps us remove whatever is not of the Lord.

Our purpose is to become more Christ-like, radiating his love and peace. The new heart and new spirit will enable us to put on Jesus.

The Lord not only wants to cleanse us from our sinfulness, but he wants to transform our hearts so that we have a greater desire and a more intense longing for a new life in God.

"You must put on that new man created in God's image, whose justice and holiness are born of truth" (Ephesians 4:24).

This desire to want to do God's will in our lives is also his gift. The spirit which he breathes into us has this transforming power:

"I will put my spirit within you and make you live by my statutes, careful to observe my decrees."

St. Paul also reminds us:

"It is God who, in his good will toward you, begets in you any measure of desire or achievement" (Philippians 2:13).

When God gifts us with this desire, we are invited to respond. God does not force himself upon us, but waits patiently.

This purification, conversion and transformation will take place within us only if we are open to the gifts of God and receptive to the power of his spirit working within us.

REVIEW OF LIFE

Do I contemplate God as he reveals to me his great desire to pardon all my sinfulness?

Do God's words assuring me of his forgiving love find a home in my heart as I ponder them?

Do I express sincere sorrow for my sins, realizing that sorrow springs from love?

How often do I thank God for his merciful love?

COLLOQUY

I give you thanks, O Lord; though you have been angry with me, your anger has abated, and you have consoled me. God, you indeed are my Savior; I am confident and unafraid. Lord, you are my strength and my courage, and you have been my Savior. With joy I will draw water at the fountain of salvation. (See Isaiah 12:1ff.)

4

Attitudinal Adjustment

"Have mercy on me, O God, in your goodness; in
the greatness of your compassion wipe out my
offense.

Thoroughly wash me from my guilt and of my sin
cleanse me.

For I acknowledge my offense, and my sin is before
me always:

'Against you only have I sinned, and done what is
evil in your sight' —

That you may be justified in your sentence, vindi-
cated when you condemn. . . .

Cleanse me of sin with hyssop, that I may be puri-
fied; wash me, and I shall be whiter than snow.

Let me hear the sounds of joy and gladness; the
bones you have crushed shall rejoice.

Turn away your face from my sins, and blot out all
my guilt.

A clean heart create for me, O God, and a steadfast
spirit renew within me.

Cast me not out from your presence, and your holy
spirit take not from me.

Give me back the joy of your salvation, and a willing spirit sustain in me" *(Psalm 51:3-6, 9-14).*

In any undertaking our attitude is of paramount importance. Attitude can spell the difference between failure
and success.

25

God looks at the dispositions of our hearts. Are we sincerely and honestly disposed to receive his forgiveness and healing?

In Psalm 51 King David helps us form the proper attitude as we approach the transcendent Lord of heaven and earth. Spending some time in praying this psalm is an ideal attitudinal adjustment to bring us to a genuine sorrow for our sins and make us more receptive to God's loving forgiveness. Listen again:

> "Have mercy on me, O God, in your goodness; in the greatness of your compassion wipe out my offense. Thoroughly wash me from my guilt and of my sin cleanse me."

Coming from a sincere heart, this prayer opens one to the floodgates of God's mercy and forgiveness.

Another essential attitude for receiving God's forgiveness is awareness of the malice of sin and the humble admission of our own sinfulness. Again the psalmist helps us:

> "For I acknowledge my offense, and my sin is before me always: 'Against you only have I sinned, and done what is evil in your sight.'"

In our time a change of attitude is of supreme importance. Many have lost a sense of sin and have become a law unto themselves, setting up private standards of morality. Pride and self-sufficiency desensitize us to our need for God. Refusal to recognize total dependence on God can lead to a culpable rejection of him. As we pray with David, we begin to discover more clearly the maliciousness of refusing God's love.

So we beg:

> "Cleanse me of sin with hyssop, that I may be purified; wash me, and I shall be whiter than snow."

Basking in God's presence brings peace and joy and the realization that God loves us and longs to forgive and heal us more than we could want it ourselves. That is the mystery of God's love.

Only sin can sever our relationship with our loving Father. We are prone to assert our own will and turn away from his love. Hence, the necessity of retaining the correct attitude toward God. May we always be aware of God's promise:

"Though your sins be like scarlet, they may become white as snow; Though they be crimson red, they may become white as wool" (Isaiah 1:18).

The contrite attitude of King David is an ideal model for us in adjusting our own attitude toward our loving Father. How fittingly we can pray in the words of the great psalmist:

"A clean heart create for me, O God, and a steadfast spirit renew within me. Cast me not out from your presence, and your holy spirit take not from me."

May his Holy Spirit keep us ever aware that sin is, in truth, a rejection of God's love. May he also keep our hearts open and receptive to the forgiving, healing, transforming power of the Father's boundless love for us.

REVIEW OF LIFE

Like David, do I turn to God and ask his forgiveness, especially at the close of each day?

Do I realize that sin is not so much the breaking of a law as a refusal to respond in love to God?

When Jesus says, "Your sins are forgiven," am I convinced that he is speaking to me personally?

Do I strive to sensitize myself to the presence and the

power of God in my life by making the daily examen of consciousness?

PRAYER

A suggested method of prayer to help us retain the proper attitude toward sinfulness is to pronounce with our heart, not just with our lips, the words "JESUS — MERCY." We can adapt these words to the rhythm of our breathing. As we inhale, pronounce the name JESUS and in exhaling, MERCY.

JESUS — MERCY   *JESUS — MERCY*

5

Love Unconditional and Enduring

"Fear not, you shall not be put to shame; you need
not blush, for you shall not be disgraced.

The shame of your youth you shall forget, the re-
proach of your widowhood no longer remember.

For he who has become your husband is your
Maker; his name is the Lord of hosts;

Your redeemer is the Holy One of Israel, called
God of all the earth.

The Lord calls you back, like a wife forsaken and
grieved in spirit,

A wife married in youth and then cast off, says
your God.

For a brief moment I abandoned you, but with
great tenderness I will take you back.

In an outburst of wrath, for a moment I hid my face
from you;

But with enduring love I take pity on you, says the
Lord, your redeemer.

This is for me like the days of Noah, when I swore
that the waters of Noah should never again de-
luge the earth;

So I have sworn not to be angry with you, or to
rebuke you.

Though the mountains leave their place and
the hills be shaken,

My love shall never leave you nor my covenant of

peace be shaken,
says the Lord, who has mercy on you" *(Isaiah 54:4ff)*.

When Adam and Eve broke their covenant with God, they were afraid and they tried to escape from God.

"When they heard the sound of the Lord God moving about in the garden at the breezy time of the day, the man and his wife hid themselves from the Lord God among the trees of the garden" *(Genesis 3:8)*.

They were afraid because they experienced guilt for the first time. They could not face God. But God came in search of them.

Their sin fragmented the love relationship which they had with him. God was disappointed. Justice demanded that this transgression not go unpunished.

However sad their plight, God assured them that eventually the human race would be redeemed and that their personal relationship with him would be restored.

This same process is repeated myriads of times in every generation. Though we turn away from God and often sever our relationship with him, our gracious Father is always in search of us sinners. Francis Thompson appropriately labelled him the Hound of Heaven, who searches for us in order to show us the way back to him.

God knows that our guilt, shame and confusion may discourage us; hence, he reassures us in his Word that he loves us in spite of our waywardness. His enduring love radiates through his message of forgiveness:

"For a brief moment I abandoned you, but with great tenderness I will take you back. In an outburst of wrath, for a moment I hid my face from you; but with enduring love I take pity on you, says the Lord, your redeemer" *(Isaiah 54:7-8)*.

The Lord's love is immutable, enduring regardless of what we have done.

Like Adam and Eve we may be filled with fear when we have failed God. We may doubt his forgiving love or the sincerity of our sorrow. If we fall into habitual sin we may be fearful, wondering if God really wants to forgive us over and over again.

Repeatedly the Father assures us that his love will never fail:

"Though the mountains leave their place and the hills be shaken, my love shall never leave you nor my covenant of peace be shaken, says the Lord, who has mercy on you."

Knowing our human weakness, our brokenness, our lack of faith, our insecurity, the Lord reaffirms that he will never abandon us, nor ever refuse to forgive us when we come to him in sincerity and sorrow. He even uses this beautiful image to reassure us:

"Can a mother forget her infant, be without tenderness for the child of her womb? Even should she forget, I will never forget you. See, upon the palms of my hands I have written your name" *(Isaiah 49:15-16)*.

This theme of God's fidelity and forgiving love runs throughout the Old Testament.

The New Testament is even a fuller revelation of this theme. As John reminds us: "For while the law was given through Moses, this enduring love came through Jesus Christ" *(John 1:17)*. The Lord's unconditional love wrought our redemption, his enduring love continues to bring us the fruits of that redemption — forgiveness and healing. "He wants none to perish but all to come to repentance" *(II Peter 3:9)*.

Am I convinced that God will never abandon me in spite of all my sinfulness?

When I realize that God loves me just as I am, how do I feel?

Do I really believe that God is saying to me: "I don't care what you have done; I love you anyway"?

How often do I reflect on the truth that God is enveloping me in his love and guiding me along the right path back to him?

PRAYER

Father, with your repentant servant David, I pray:

"A clean heart create for me, O God, and a steadfast spirit renew within me. Cast me not out from your presence, and your holy spirit take not from me. Give me back the joy of your salvation, and a willing spirit sustain in me" (Psalm 51:12ff).

Sacramental Encounter

6

A Personal Encounter With Jesus

"Receive the Holy Spirit.
If you forgive men's sins,
they are forgiven them;
if you hold them bound,
they are held bound."
(John 20:22-23).

After his resurrection Jesus becomes a "Consoler." On the very day of his rising, Jesus brought great comfort and consolation to his followers and was delighted to greet them in the upper room with "Peace be with you." As the disciples rejoiced in seeing the Lord alive, Jesus said again: "Peace be with you."

Peace is a divine gift, won by Jesus with his victory on the cross. As the fruit of love, peace is dispensed to us personally as a special fruit of the Holy Spirit *(Galatians 5:22)* through the sacramental channel of reconciliation. Peace comes when we realize that we are reconciled with our heavenly Father and that no burden of sin separates us from him. Little wonder that this rite is indeed the Sacrament of pardon, reconciliation and peace.

When Jesus completed his redemptive mission, our relationship with the Father was reestablished, our friendship restored, never again to be completely severed.

By his death and rising Jesus redeemed the human race. We now enjoy the capability of receiving the gift of divine life which he wishes to share with us. In this gift Jesus dwells within us through the power of the Holy Spirit. What greater joy and consolation could he bring us!

Jesus wants to give us an even greater measure of peace and satisfaction. His redemption is open to every person. This fact may make his redemptive work seem rather universal and impersonal. Jesus wants us to encounter him personally to assure each one of us his forgiving, healing, redeeming love. He is the transcendent God of the universe, but he is also each one's personal God, wanting to deepen his life in us whenever we meet him in this Sacrament of his mercy and compassion.

On the very day of the resurrection, Jesus instituted the Sacrament of forgiveness. In the upper room where Jesus met the apostles, he empowered them to administer forgiveness in his name. The work of sanctification, in the power of the Holy Spirit, was entrusted to them.

> "He breathed on them and said: 'Receive the Holy Spirit. If you forgive men's sins, they are forgiven them; if you hold them bound, they are held bound.' "

The sanctification of the Church is the special mission of the Holy Spirit. He channels forgiveness and healing to us personally through this sacramental rite.

Each time we receive the Sacrament of Penance, Jesus, who is dwelling with us in his resurrected, exalted life, deepens his life in us. He is there to forgive and to heal.

There is still another important aspect to receiving the Sacrament of Penance. Each time we encounter Jesus in this Sacrament, we acknowledge we are sinners in need of forgiveness. We express our need of Jesus as Savior and Redeemer. This pleases Jesus because we permit him to fulfill his redemptive role. We ask him to be our Savior. He is delighted to be so.

Furthermore, we rejoice the heart of Jesus when we seek him in this Sacrament because we are open and receptive to the conversion and transformation he wishes to effect in us. The Sacrament of Penance is the Lord's special gift to us, his wayward children. Auricular confession is a personal gift to us individually. Here Jesus waits for us to come to him.

We show appreciation for a gift by using it for its intended purpose. Each time we receive the Sacrament of Penance we thank the Lord for his gift of forgiveness and healing. There is no better way to express our gratitude.

REVIEW OF LIFE

When I receive the Sacrament of Penance, do I realize that I am encountering the Risen Jesus?

Do I appreciate the fact that Jesus comes to me in this Sacrament to assure me personally that I am forgiven?

Am I faithful in meeting Jesus regularly in this channel of pardon and peace?

What is my reaction to the truth that Jesus wants to forgive me more than I myself could even want forgiveness?

COLLOQUY

Lord Jesus, how many times I have encountered you in this Sacrament. Never once did you refuse or even hesitate to forgive me regardless of what I had done. On the contrary, how readily you responded: "Your sins are forgiven you." Give me a humble and contrite heart filled with the peace and joy which only you can give.

7

Healing Love

"Come to me, all you who are weary and find life burdensome, and I will refresh you. Take my yoke upon your shoulders and learn from me, for I am gentle and humble of heart. Your souls will find rest, for my yoke is easy and my burden light" *(Matthew 11:28ff)*.

How often should I receive the Sacrament of Penance? This question arises because we often lack proper appreciation of the far-reaching fruits of this Sacrament of God's pardon and peace.

Some think of this Sacrament merely as a means of having our sins forgiven, necessary only if we have had the misfortune to fall into serious sin.

The question — How often should one receive the Sacrament of Penance? — can be best answered by asking ourselves another question. How often do we need healing? Jesus is not only our Redeemer, he is also our Healer. At times we may need inner healing even more than we need forgiveness.

In some instances we are not able to amend our lives until we are healed interiorly. Healing gets to the root of our problem or weakness.

Jesus invites us to come to him if we are weary or find life burdensome. Our routine duties may become monotonous. We may lose interest in our work. We may be just plain tired.

Jesus can and does heal us by giving us new inspiration and renewed motivation so that we better understand what he wills for us. He can change our whole attitude. These duties, which sometimes seem boring, may be our stairway into our eternal union with him. This realization helps us tackle them with new enthusiasm and greater zeal.

If we find ourselves critical and judgmental toward others, and not able to accept them, we become quite uncharitable. Resolutions to overcome this attitude seem short-lived and, when broken, create a greater sense of guilt.

Here is where we need the Lord's healing. We need to discern the cause of our uncharitableness. Are we jealous or envious of that person? Have we permitted a resentment to build within us?

If we are insecure we see others as a threat to us and become defensive or react unkindly toward them. There are many other reasons why we are uncharitable. These indicate that we need inner healing before we can overcome our uncharitableness.

Jesus can and will heal us. However, his healing depends upon our disposition. We must ask ourselves: Do I really want to be healed?

When Jesus met the man at the Sheep Pool, Bethesda, he seemed to ask a rather obvious question. This man was ill for thirty-eight years, yet Jesus asked: "Do you want to be healed?" (John 5:1ff).

This man probably was a professional beggar. According to the customs of the times, he was permitted to beg for his livelihood. If he were healed he would have to change his mode of living and even earn his own livelihood. Jesus' question was very much in order.

Jesus addresses the same question to us: "Do you want to be healed?" He instituted the Sacrament with its divine healing potential, but he never forces himself upon us. Rather, he waits for us to respond to his invitation that he heal us. And pleased he is when we do so.

Regarding the Sacrament of Penance, do we question our need for healing, or are we satisfied that we can handle all our problems? Do we find it inconvenient or embarrassing to seek the Sacrament of healing? Do we keep Jesus waiting? If so, Jesus continues to wait. That is the mystery of his love.

REVIEW OF LIFE

In moments of impatience, or when I feel anger welling up within me, do I turn to Jesus with a brief prayer: "Lord, heal me"?

If I am harboring a grudge or resentment, do I hear Jesus asking: "Do you want to be healed?"

When I receive the Sacrament of Penance, do I also ask for a general or a specific healing?

Do I keep myself aware that Jesus wants to heal me interiorly, so that he can work more freely and more fruitfully in me?

COLLOQUY

Jesus, during your earthly sojourn you wanted to be known as a healer. I know that you are the same yesterday, today and forever. Fill every fibre of my being with your healing presence and power. Help me to be open to your healing love, and rid me of any obstacles which may be interfering with your working freely within me. Amen.

8

Sins of Omission

''Then he [Jesus] will say to those on his left: 'Out of my sight, you condemned, into that everlasting fire prepared for the devil and his angels! I was hungry and you gave me no food, I was thirsty and you gave me no drink. I was away from home and you gave me no welcome, naked and you gave me no clothing. I was ill and in prison and you did not come to comfort me.' Then they in turn will ask: 'Lord, when did we see you hungry or thirsty or away from home or naked, or ill or in prison and not attend you in your needs?' He will answer them: 'I assure you, as often as you neglected to do it to one of these least ones, you neglected to do it to me.' These will go off to eternal punishment and the just to eternal life'' *(Matthew 25:41ff)*.

There is a natural tendency to recall sins of commission. We seem to be more aware of them than of sins of omission. But failing to perform duties, neglecting to respond to another's needs when we ought to, is also sinful. These are sins of omission.

In this area we often rationalize and excuse ourselves because we do not want to become involved. This is a refusal or a failure to manifest our Christian love.

In narrating the story of the Last Judgment, Jesus was severe in his condemnation. He condemned those on the left for their lack of responding to others in need. He even consigned them "into that everlasting fire prepared for the devil and his angels" because they neglected to show loving concern for the hungry, the thirsty, the naked, the sick and those away from home or those imprisoned.

Here Jesus was referring to only a sampling of the many ways we can love or neglect our neighbors. These are just a few of the ways in which we can offend by neglect. There are countless other ways as we go through the happenings of every day.

In the account of the Good Samaritan, Jesus implicitly condemned the priest and Levite who happened to go down the same road along which "the man who fell prey to robbers" had traveled. "They stripped him, beat him, and then went off leaving him half-dead." Both the Jewish priest and the Levite could have helped the man, but failed to do so *(Luke 10:25ff)*.

As we reflect on the Gospel account of the Rich Man and Lazarus *(Luke 16:19ff)*, we are not aware of any reason why the rich man should be condemned and "tortured in these flames," other than that he neglected to provide sufficiently for others. His sin was one of omission — neglecting to share his goods to help others like the beggar.

We can become oblivious to the needs of others. This is a failure to love as Jesus commanded. Of the various levels of love, he led us to the first when he said:

"You shall love your neighbor as yourself" *(Matthew 22:39)*.

Jesus made loving concern the badge of discipleship:

"This is how all will know you for my disciples: your love for one another" *(John 13:35)*.

We can reach out in loving concern to others in myriad ways.

Sometimes a person who is troubled, anxious or worried simply needs a friend to listen with love and concern.

We can neglect to smile, to greet another person kindly.

41

A visit, a phone call to a sick person or a shut-in can be an expression of concern.

Giving our spouse or children time and attention when they need it can also be an expression of love.

Perhaps our sin is not so much what we have done, but rather what we have failed to do.

REVIEW OF LIFE

Do I reflect on the day just passed in order to discover whether or not I have omitted any opportunity to show loving concern for others?

Am I alert to commend others or to thank them for the good they have done?

Do I convey the impression that I am too busy to visit, to listen or to help others?

Do I try to experience what other persons may be experiencing so that I can relate to them with loving concern?

COLLOQUY

Lord Jesus, let your words ". . . as often as you did it for one of my least brothers, you did it for me" ring in my heart. Help me to recognize you in all the persons who daily cross my path. Fill me with your love, so that I may never neglect to reach out to others.

Come
and See

9

Dinner Date

"There was a certain Pharisee who invited Jesus to dine with him. Jesus went to the Pharisee's home and reclined to eat. A woman known in the town to be a sinner learned that he was dining in the Pharisee's home. She brought in a vase of perfumed oil and stood behind him at his feet, weeping so that her tears fell upon his feet. Then she wiped them with her hair, kissing them and perfuming them with the oil. When his host, the Pharisee, saw this, he said to himself, 'If this man were a prophet, he would know who and what sort of woman this is that touches him — that she is a sinner.' In answer to his thoughts, Jesus said to him, 'Simon, I have something to propose to you.' 'Teacher,' he said, 'speak.'

" 'Two men owed money to a certain money-lender; one owed a total of five hundred coins, the other fifty. Since neither was able to repay, he wrote off both debts. Which of them was more grateful to him?' Simon answered, 'He, I presume, to whom he remitted the larger sum.' Jesus said to him, 'You are right.' Turning then to the woman, he said to Simon: 'You see this woman? I came to your home and you provided me with no water for my feet. She has washed my feet with her tears and wiped them with her hair. You gave me no kiss, but she has not ceased kissing my feet since I entered. You did not anoint my head with oil, but she has anointed my feet with perfume. I tell you, that is why her many sins are forgiven — because of her great love. Little is forgiven the one whose love is small.'

"He said to her then, 'Your sins are forgiven'; at which his fellow guests began to ask among themselves, 'Who is this that he even forgives sins?' Meanwhile he said to the woman, 'Your faith has been your salvation. Now go in peace' " *(Luke 7:36ff)*.

In this touching scene, Jesus is confronting two sinners — one a nameless woman, the other, Simon, a self-righteous Pharisee. Even though their dispositions are diametrically different, Jesus reaches out with compassionate love to both of them. Be alert to all the nuances as Jesus deals with both of these sinners.

At first we may wonder at the woman's presence in the home of the Pharisee. Was she an uninvited guest? Did she crash this dinner party? Was there a possibility that Simon might have encouraged her presence in order to embarrass Jesus, or to try him, since Pharisees did not come near to sinners, nor did they have any dealings with them.

The presence of the woman was understandable. According to the customs of that day, people for the most part dined out-of-doors, patio-style as we would call it. This fact would give the woman easy access to Simon's house.

It was also a custom that when a rabbi was invited to dine in someone's home, anyone could come to hear the words of wisdom which the rabbi might speak.

It is possible, too, that Jesus might have been expounding on the loving mercy and the great compassion of the Father and how eager he is to forgive sinners.

Jesus' words or his magnetic personality might have overwhelmed this "woman known in the town to be a sinner." She was so overcome that her tears flowed uncon-

45

trollably. As her copious tears washed the feet of Jesus, she had no way to dry them except to use her hair as a towel. This was another breach — since women in that day were not permitted to expose their hair.

Simon's reaction took shape immediately in his mind. Quickly he sat in judgment on Jesus. He felt certain that he had trapped Jesus, for he thought: "If this man were a prophet, he would know what sort of woman this is that touches him — that she is a sinner."

Simon was a Pharisee, one of the strictest sect among the Jews. They were legalists who observed the multiplicity of rules and regulations of the law, as well as the myriad interpretations which they themselves devised.

Like all Pharisees, Simon believed that the exact observance of the law would justify him and thus he would be saved. For this reason Simon was self-righteous. He considered himself a good man; therefore, he did not need God's forgiveness. Yet he felt justified in condemning this poor woman whom he considered a sinner. Along with her, he was condemning Jesus for accepting her ministrations.

With a simple little example Jesus explained how important were the proper dispositions for receiving God's mercy and also our need for gratitude. Jesus spoke volumes when he said: "I tell you, that is why her many sins are forgiven — because of her great love. Little is forgiven the one whose love is small."

Simon did not love enough to perform the ordinary courtesies which were accorded any guest. He did not love enough to want to be forgiven and healed.

REVIEW OF LIFE

Does the self-righteous Pharisee in me always insist on justifying my own actions and attitudes?

Am I quick to judge others?

How do I feel when I hear Jesus saying to me: "Your sins are forgiven you"?

Have I ever been moved to tears when I hear the Father say: "I don't care what you have done; I love you anyway"?

COLLOQUY

Lord Jesus, in this Gospel account, you scored a direct hit. How well I fit into Simon's sandals as I justify my own faults and failures and consider myself better than others, especially those I think are sinners. In spite of my pharisaical pride you continue to love me. Teach me to love as intensely as this woman did, so that I may be forgiven also.

10

Raising the Roof

"While he [Jesus] was delivering God's word to them, some people arrived bringing a paralyzed man to him. The four who carried him were unable to bring him to Jesus because of the crowd, so they began to open up the roof over the spot where Jesus was. When they had made a hole, they let down the mat on which the paralytic was lying. When Jesus saw their faith, he said to the paralyzed man, 'My son, your sins are forgiven.' Now some of the scribes were sitting there asking themselves: 'Why does the man talk in that way? He commits blasphemy! Who can forgive sins except God alone?' Jesus was immediately aware of their reasoning, though they kept it to themselves, and he said to them: 'Why do you harbor these thoughts? Which is easier, to say to the paralytic, "Your sins are forgiven," or to say, "Stand up, pick up your mat, and walk again"? That you may know that the Son of Man has authority on earth to forgive sins' (he said to the paralyzed man), 'I command you: Stand up! Pick up your mat and go home.' The man stood and picked up his mat and went outside in the sight of everyone. They were awestruck; all gave praise to God, saying, 'We have never seen anything like this!' " (Mark 2:3ff).

Jesus appeals to us to have faith in him. He wants us to place our trust and confidence in him. How pleased Jesus is when he finds faith in him! How chilled he becomes when that faith is lacking.

In this incident of the paralytic at Capernaum, the evangelists are eager to point out that Jesus was touched by the faith of the men who carried the paralyzed man. This faith moved Jesus to heal the crippled man. "Seeing their faith, Jesus said: 'My son, your sins are forgiven.' "

On another occasion the evangelist says pathetically: "He [Jesus] did not work many miracles there because of their lack of faith" *(Matthew 13:58)*.

The people who carried the paralytic must have had great faith and confidence in Jesus. With considerable effort they brought the man to Jesus, even removing part of the roof covering. We do not know whether they carried the man a short distance or from afar. We do know, however, that their kindness and trust pleased Jesus very much.

Secondly, they were not to be daunted by the crowd surrounding Jesus. When they could not get through the crowd hemming Jesus in, they went up on the roof and let the man down through the opening they had made. This, too, speaks of the persistence of their faith. Faith and love will always find a way. Faith and love also generate great confidence and trust.

The compassionate heart of Jesus always touched the whole person. Apparently they were hoping that Jesus would heal this man's paralysis, which he did, but in the process he also healed the whole man. "My son, your sins are forgiven."

Jesus was certainly aware that he would be criticized by the spies who were always dogging his footsteps. Jesus could have ignored them, but he wanted the rest of the audience to know that he had the power to forgive sins, and that he loved enough to want to forgive.

Jesus challenged his enemies. He wanted them to know

that he knew what they were thinking; hence he asked them:

"Why do you harbor these thoughts? Which is easier, to say to the paralytic: 'Your sins are forgiven,' or to say, 'Stand up, pick up your mat, and walk again'?"

In reality Jesus was appealing to his enemies. He was striving to convince them to recognize the signs he was performing as coming through his divine power. He was trying to enkindle a spark of faith in the hearts of the scribes by demonstrating his power.

" 'That you may know that the Son of Man has authority on earth to forgive sins ' (he said to the paralyzed man), 'I command you: Stand up! Pick up your mat and go home.' "

This is precisely what the healed paralytic did.

"The man stood and picked up his mat and went outside in the sight of everyone."

Jesus did not heal this man, nor other persons, primarily to manifest his divine power, but rather his tender and loving concern. This is evident in part from the fact that he requested many persons whom he healed not to mention their healing to others.

In this incident, Jesus wanted to prove that he had authority to forgive sins. He demonstrated it conclusively not only for his enemies but for us as well.

When we come with faith to Jesus, he cannot be outdone in generosity. He not only forgives our sins, but he often heals us of the cause of our failings. In order to be healed, we must be open and receptive to what he wants to effect within us. Being open is not always easy. We need to implore God for that grace.

This Gospel episode also reminds us that we have an obligation in love to bring others to Jesus for his forgiveness and healing. Jesus was pleased at the faith of the men who carried the paralytic. He will be greatly pleased by our faith and zeal in leading others to him.

"Remember this: the person who brings a sinner back from his way will save his soul from death and cancel a multitude of sins" (James 5:20).

We can lead others to Jesus, especially those in our own family, by our prayers and our example. As we make use of this Rite of Reconciliation, we are showing others our appreciation of this channel of healing and forgiveness.

We manifest our faith by encouraging others to meet Jesus in the Sacrament of pardon and peace. If necessary, accompany them if they are fearful or hesitant.

REVIEW OF LIFE

Do I doubt that Jesus will continue to forgive me in spite of my recurring infidelities?

Do I speak appreciatively to others of the Sacrament of Penance?

When was the last time I encouraged a person to receive this Sacrament, and did I volunteer to accompany such a person, or instruct him or her in the method of approaching the Sacrament?

Do I tell the Lord how grateful I am for coming to me personally in this Sacrament to assure me personally and individually of his loving forgiveness?

COLLOQUY

Jesus, Lord and Healer, your heart must have been light and filled with joy when you saw how trustingly these four people, with great effort, brought the paralytic and begged your healing for him. Help me to remove any lack of appreciation, any preoccupation or hesitation, any barrier or obstacle, which hinders or delays me from encountering you in this Rite of Reconciliation where you patiently wait to offer me forgiveness and healing, pardon and peace. Amen.

11

Pharisee and Tax Collector

"He then spoke this parable addressed to those who believed in their own self-righteousness while holding everyone else in contempt: 'Two men went up to the temple to pray; one was a Pharisee, the other a tax collector. The Pharisee with head unbowed prayed in this fashion: "I give you thanks, O God, that I am not like the rest of men — grasping, crooked, adulterous — or even like this tax collector. I fast twice a week. I pay tithes on all I possess." The other man, however, kept his distance, not even daring to raise his eyes to heaven. All he did was beat his breast and say, "O God, be merciful to me, a sinner." Believe me, this man went home from the temple justified but the other did not. For everyone who exalts himself shall be humbled while he who humbles himself shall be exalted' " *(Luke 18:9ff)*.

Jesus was a teacher par excellence. With an economy of words, he outlined the dispositions required for obtaining God's forgiveness. With the brevity characteristic of the Gospel, St. Luke relates this episode pedagogically in a parable.

The Pharisees' way of life was the exact observance of the law with all its minutiae. They followed strictly the thousands of interpretations of the law. Most of these were their own interpretations of the law.

They believed that they were holy and justified by this strict observance of the traditions of the law. If they obeyed all this legalism, they thought themselves sinless, and therefore much better than others who did not have the time to study the law, much less live its every detail.

In their pride they judged every other person to be a sinner. They even accused Jesus of violating the law; hence they concluded he could not be a prophet.

This same pride urged the Pharisee who went to the temple to pray to inform God how good he was because he obeyed every detail of the law. His proud heart was not open to God's forgiving love, nor did he think that he needed forgiveness.

On the other hand, we have the antithesis in the tax collector, of whom Jesus says:

> "The other man, however, kept his distance, not even daring to raise his eyes to heaven. All he did was beat his breast and say, 'O God, be merciful to me, a sinner.' "

In any age tax collectors are not the most beloved people. In Jesus' time the attitude of the people toward tax collectors was even worse. The Jewish people were extremely nationalistic. They believed that God would not permit them to be enslaved long by any occupying government.

At this time the Romans had conquered them and were occupying their country. Characteristically, as a conquering nation, Rome imposed heavy taxes upon the Jews. This embittered the Jews all the more against the Romans. Their method of collecting taxes increased the hatred of the people toward the tax collectors also. It seems that certain men were appointed to collect a specific amount of taxes from the people, payable to the Romans. The tax collector's remuneration was only what he could collect over and above the amount demanded by the conquerors. Some tax collectors were dishonest and tried to feather their own nests. They were hated and despised. They were even considered traitors to their own people.

On the other hand, Jesus understood their plight. His contemplative heart could see the interior dispositions of some of these social outcasts. How often he championed their cause!

In this Gospel episode Jesus reads the heart of the tax collector. He sees the humble, contrite disposition of the man. What a tremendous endorsement Jesus gave him:

"Believe me, this man went home from the temple justified but the other did not. For everyone who exalts himself shall be humbled while he who humbles himself shall be exalted."

REVIEW OF LIFE

Does this Gospel narrative cause me some discomfort?

Is my attitude more like the Pharisee than like that of the tax collector?

Do I, like the Pharisee, sit in judgment on others?

Does the Pharisee in me consider myself better than others?

PRAYER

Loving Father, when I am tempted to see the wrongdoing of another, let me remember: But for your grace, there go I. With the tax collector I pray: "O God, be merciful to me, a sinner."

12

Hieroglyphics in the Dust

"The scribes and the Pharisees led a woman forward who had been caught in adultery. They made her stand in front of everyone. 'Teacher,' they said to him, 'this woman has been caught in the act of adultery. In the law, Moses ordered such women to be stoned. What do you have to say about the case?' (They were posing this question to trap him, so that they could have something to accuse him of.) Jesus bent down and started tracing on the ground with his finger. When they persisted in their questioning, he straightened up and said to them, 'Let the man among you who has no sin be the first to cast a stone at her.' A second time he bent down and wrote on the ground. Then the audience drifted away one by one, beginning with the elders. This left him alone with the woman, who continued to stand there before him. Jesus finally straightened up and said to her, 'Woman, where did they all disappear to? Has no one condemned you?' 'No one, sir,' she answered. Jesus said, 'Nor do I condemn you. You may go. But from now on, avoid this sin' " (John 8:3ff).

The dramatis personae of this Gospel scene presents a strange situation. The end result manifests Jesus' loving concern and compassion. He did not condemn, nor condone. He appealed to his enemies, hoping they would recognize their own perfidy. In the end he forgave and encouraged the woman to avoid this sin.

Let us linger with the happenings.

"The scribes and the Pharisees led a woman forward who had been caught in adultery. They made her stand in front of everyone."

They did so endeavoring to trap Jesus. Obviously there were two people on trial; this woman as well as Jesus. If Jesus condemned her they would have cause to point out his lack of compassion and forgiveness which he had preached incessantly. On the other hand, if Jesus pardoned her, he would have been accused of violating the Mosaic Law.

The hypocrisy of her accusers was so apparent. Where was her partner in crime? Why was not the man involved brought to trial? If this woman was "caught in the act of adultery," surely his identity was known.

In our humanness we have a propensity to project our own guilt or blame on someone else. Were these scribes and Pharisees trying to cover their own guilt? Be that as it may, "Jesus bent down and started tracing on the ground with his finger." Jesus did this perhaps to manifest his utter disdain and total disinterestedness in this trap in which they were trying to ensnare him.

Jesus ignored them, which gave them an opportunity to leave and not risk having their own sinfulness exposed. However, they were too intent on their deception to take the hint.

"When they persisted in their questioning, he straightened up and said to them, 'Let the man among you who has no sin be the first to cast a stone at her.' A second time he bent down and wrote on the ground."

Fearing exposure of their sinfulness, "the audience drifted away one by one, beginning with the elders."

When they had all gone, Jesus said to her:

" 'Woman, where did they all disappear to? Has no one condemned you?' 'No one, sir,' she answered. Jesus said, 'Nor do I condemn you. You may go. But from now on, avoid this sin.' "

The compassion of Jesus dominates this whole narrative. Jesus could have exposed his enemies by revealing their own personal sins. As his enemies were trying to ensnare him, Jesus did respond with firmness, but also with love which they refused. They left unrepentant and unforgiven, whereas the woman left in peace and joy, knowing that she was forgiven.

It is characteristic of our human nature to want to excuse ourselves when we fall. We often allege that if certain conditions were present, we would not have fallen.

When we criticize others or point out what we think are their faults and failures, we are really saying, "He or she has these shortcomings, but I do not." Usually what we see as faults in another are our own weaknesses which we may or may not recognize. This is why we readily recognize these faults and failures in others.

Furthermore, even if another person is doing something which may be objectively sinful, we can humbly admit: "But for the grace of God, there go I."

This nameless woman was humiliated and embarrassed, but she was also sincerely contrite. Jesus read her heart and his forgiveness poured out upon her.

REVIEW OF LIFE

Did Jesus scratch on the ground while I was pointing an accusing finger at a brother or sister?

Do I humbly admit my own failures without making excuses for them?

Do I recognize my own self-righteousness on so many

occasions?

As Jesus reveals more about himself in this Gospel event, does it bring me into a deeper appreciation of his merciful compassion?

COLLOQUY

Merciful and compassionate Jesus, in this Gospel scene I recognize myself on so many occasions. I am willing to point out the shortcomings of others while advertently or inadvertently trying to conceal my own. Jesus, you are so patient with me. Help me to recognize my true self and humbly turn to you for healing and forgiveness.

13

Strayed Sheep Found

"The tax collectors and sinners were all gathering around to hear him, at which the Pharisees and the scribes murmured, 'This man welcomes sinners and eats with them.' Then he addressed this parable to them: 'Who among you, if he has a hundred sheep and loses one of them, does not leave the ninety-nine in the wasteland and follow the lost one until he finds it? And when he finds it, he puts it on his shoulders in jubilation. Once arrived home, he invites friends and neighbors in and says to them, "Rejoice with me because I have found my lost sheep." I tell you, there will likewise be more joy in heaven over one repentant sinner than over ninety-nine righteous people who have no need to repent" *(Luke 15:1ff)*.

Does the Lord really care about lost sheep — those persons who have strayed away from the path he mapped out for all his faithful followers? Does he continue to love those people who have sinned and continue to refuse his love? Would the Lord care about me if I had the misfortune to sin seriously? Would he be angry and want to punish me?

Jesus was the best of teachers. He answered all these questions and the doubts and fears which accompany them in one touching parable.

Jesus painted a picture of himself and revealed the

solicitude of his heart by identifying himself as a shepherd in search of one lost sheep. He would leave the ninety-nine in the wasteland and follow the lost one until he finds it.

Furthermore, Jesus would not drive it back to the flock in anger at its straying away. No, "he puts it on his shoulders in jubilation." Jesus goes on to say that he would invite friends and neighbors to rejoice with him because he had found a lost sheep. In the Scriptures when there is a conversion there is always rejoicing.

Then Jesus made his point — the punch line if you will:

"I tell you, there will likewise be more joy in heaven over one repentant sinner than over ninety-nine righteous people who have no need to repent."

What joy and consolation all of us can feel knowing that Jesus loves us so much that he is always in search of us. If a sinner would doubt the Lord's forgiveness, all that he would have to do is to listen at the very core of his being to the Father saying:

"You are precious in my eyes and glorious, and because I love you" *(Isaiah 43:4)*.

Or again:

"I will never forget you. See, upon the palms of my hands I have written your name" *(Isaiah 49:15-16)*.

Can we doubt God's infinite, compassionate love wanting to forgive us if we but accept it? God is really saying: "I don't care what you have done; I love you anyway. I love you just as you are."

We cannot exhaustively comprehend that kind of love, but God is mystery:

"My heart is overwhelmed, my pity is stirred. . . . For I am God and not man, the Holy One present among you; I will not let the flames consume you" *(Hosea 11:8-9)*.

Francis Thompson has endeavored to capture some of the insistent love of God for sinners in his famous poem "The Hound of Heaven." As the Scriptures have before him, the poet tries to show the futility of trying to escape the overwhelming love of God for sinners. The dedication of the poem is itself a prayer:

To
The Hound of Heaven
that his pursuit of our souls
may be swift and brief.

REVIEW OF LIFE

Do I worry about my sinfulness by doubting God's forgiving love in my case?

Am I anxious about past failings, wondering if I was sufficiently disposed to receive God's forgiveness?

Do I rejoice when some strayed sheep returns to the fold?

Do I encourage and help others to return, especially if they are not knowledgeable about the New Rite of the Sacrament of Penance?

COLLOQUY

Jesus, like the lost sheep, in doing my own thing, I, too, have strayed far off the path which you mapped out for me. Thank you for being the Good Shepherd always in pursuit of me. Thank you for your tenderness in taking me back into your fold so that I may have that life which you came to give and have it to the full.

Never release my hand from your hand, lest I wander off again.

Yes, Jesus, there is joy in heaven over one repentant sinner, and my heart, too, is singing with joy.

14

The Shorter Road Home

"Jesus said to them: 'A man had two sons. The younger of them said to his father, "Father, give me the share of the estate that is coming to me." So the father divided up the property.

" 'Some days later this younger son collected all his belongings and went off to a distant land, where he squandered his money on dissolute living. After he had spent everything, a great famine broke out in that country and he was in dire need. So he attached himself to one of the propertied class of the place, who sent him to his farm to take care of the pigs.

" 'He longed to fill his belly with the husks that were fodder for the pigs, but no one made a move to give him anything. Coming to his senses at last, he said: "How many hired hands at my father's place have more than enough to eat, while here I am starving! I will break away and return to my father, and say to him, Father, I have sinned against God and against you; I no longer deserve to be called your son. Treat me like one of your hired hands." With that he set off for his father's house. While he was still a long way off, his father caught sight of him and was deeply moved. He ran out to meet him, threw his arms around his neck, and kissed him. The son said to him, "Father, I have sinned against God and against you; I no longer deserve to be called your son." The father said to his servants: "Quick! bring out the finest robe and put it on him; put a ring on his finger and shoes on his feet. Take the fatted calf and kill it. Let us eat and celebrate because this son of mine was dead and has come back to life. He was lost and is found." Then the celebration began' " (Luke 15:11-24).

Everyone seems to agree that the title of this parable is a misnomer. It should be called the Prodigal Father, yet popular usage continues to dub it the Prodigal Son.

Jesus had many reasons for telling this parable. It is intended for many of us and it teaches us some valuable lessons.

Jesus must have taken delight in narrating this story, because he was always anxious to reveal more and more about the love and compassion the Father has for us. It does speak eloquently to us who may at times have been his wayward sons and daughters.

The words which seem to capsulize this portion of the parable for me are the expression of the younger son: "Father, I have sinned against God and against you." "I have sinned" bespeaks the humble disposition of the wayward son.

The younger son embodies within himself all the elements of sin and the misery caused by sin. He was selfish in demanding his share of the estate with no thought of the hardship he was imposing upon the rest of the family. His self-gratification also led him into dissolute living. All of which dragged him into the gutter of misery and unhappiness where he tasted the ashes of disillusionment.

However, when he got hungry enough, a conversion started to take place within him. He came to his senses and resolved to "break away" and return to his father.

He did so with some natural misgivings. He did not

know how he would be received. Furthermore, it took great courage and humility to face his father and brother once again; nevertheless "he set off for his father's house."

Jesus wants us to observe the father's reactions when he sees his wayward son coming back home. "He ran out to meet him, threw his arms around him and kissed him."

The father did not give his son an opportunity to make his confession. Instead he immediately instructed the servants to prepare a big feast after putting on him the finest robe, a ring on his finger and shoes on his feet.

The father accepted his son without any kind of confession or commitment. Nor did he demand any apology or explanation.

Jesus told us this parable to assure us that the Father will receive us in exactly the same manner if we have the misfortune to stray from him. The conditions are not all that stringent. Genuine sorrow forms a humble disposition which makes us receptive to God's loving forgiveness. For the younger son, the road home was much shorter than for the elder brother. The younger son recognized his sinfulness, was deeply sorry and was sufficiently humble to seek forgiveness.

With the younger son we are called to recognize that sin is an expression of our selfishness. We want our way, our desire, our plans, our pleasure with little or no thought of others.

Realizing that sinfulness has separated us from the Lord, we are invited to humbly acknowledge our guilt, be willing to admit it and be moved to do something about it.

When we are thus disposed we can be assured that the Father's love will be reaching out to us, ready and eager to embrace us. Someone expressed it in these words: If we, with all our sinfulness, take one step toward our compassionate Father, he will take the other ninety-nine steps toward us.

REVIEW OF LIFE

Do I see my selfishness as the cause of my sinfulness?

Do I humbly admit to myself, to God and, if necessary, to others my own sinfulness?

Like the younger son, when I come to my senses do I swallow my pride and take the road back?

Do I show by my example how important and fruitful is the Sacrament of Reconciliation?

COLLOQUY

Father, how much I am like the younger son, vulnerable to all the snares of selfishness and self-centeredness which sidetrack me away from your loving presence. Forgive me once again, Father. Heal the scars of my sinfulness and grant that I may rest secure in your loving presence.

15

The Longer Road Home

"Meanwhile the elder son was out on the land. As he neared the house on his way home, he heard the sound of music and dancing. He called one of the servants and asked him the reason for the dancing and the music. The servant answered, 'Your brother is home, and your father has killed the fatted calf because he has him back in good health.' The son grew angry at this and would not go in; but his father came out and began to plead with him.

"He said to his father in reply: 'For years now I have slaved for you. I never disobeyed one of your orders, yet you never gave me so much as a kid goat to celebrate with my friends. Then, when this son of yours returns after having gone through your property with loose women, you kill the fatted calf for him.'

" 'My son,' replied the father, 'you are with me always, and everything I have is yours. But we had to celebrate and rejoice! This brother of yours was dead, and has come back to life. He was lost, and is found' " *(Luke 15:25-32)*.

This is one of Jesus' unfinished parables. What happened to the elder son and brother? First the servants went out to appeal to him to come and join in the celebration of the homecoming of his brother. The elder brother grew angry at this and would not go in. His father came out and began to plead with him to join in the celebration. The words which seem to me to reecho throughout this portion of the parable are: "I have slaved for you." There is little or no love reflected in that expression.

Did the elder brother finally relent and welcome his wayward brother back to the fold and family? Did he remain in this state of anger and continue to reject his contrite brother? No further details are given in the Gospel.

If the elder brother did remain obstinate and unforgiving, his road back was much longer than the road which the younger brother travelled. The elder brother was angry and adamant. He was not open and receptive. He refused to forgive his younger brother even though the younger brother humbly begged his pardon.

Jesus did not finish this parable, because he wants us to look at ourselves. Is our attitude at times similar to that of the elder brother? Do we find it hard to forgive and forget? Do we even refuse to forgive? Do we refuse to speak to a certain person or persons?

How do we feel about a sinner who has returned to God? Do we mistrust him or her? Do we allege an ulterior or selfish reason for his or her returning? What is our general attitude toward sinners, or people we consider sinners? Are we inclined to take the attitude of the elder brother?

A movie entitled *Fiesta* portrays the scene of this parable. In the movie the father goes out to the elder son to plead with him to come in and forgive his younger brother. The elder son, who is fixing the fence out on the farm, becomes so angry that he slams the hammer into a fence post, almost breaking it off.

The father remains calm and unruffled. He quietly proposes a riddle to his son. He said: "I am a father. I have two sons. You are my son, yet you have no brother?"

The father quietly and slowly reverses his steps and walks down the lane toward the house. The son pauses in his work to watch his father walk away with heavy steps.

Like every movie *Fiesta* must have a happy ending. Yes, the elder brother finally comes to the celebration. All the music, dancing and singing stops. The brothers observe each other rather uncertainly, then they embrace and the celebration begins with a new tempo of joviality.

The movie portrayed the infinite patience of our heavenly Father. The natural father was dealing with two sinners. His patience and strength endured, and eventually wrought the reconciliation.

Our loving Father in heaven is so patient with all of us. He welcomes sinners with open arms when they return to him. He understands our brokenness and how difficult it is for us to forgive on some occasions. He waits. His patience is infinite.

His grace finally touches the unforgiving heart and peace and tranquility are restored.

By pondering and reflecting upon this parable we gain new insights into the heart of the Father and the boundless compassion and mercy with which the Father waits for our return.

God is light. By drawing closer to him we can understand our own attitude more clearly. God is love. The more we experience his love for us, the easier it is for us to reach out in loving forgiveness to others.

REVIEW OF LIFE

Is my attitude ever that of the elder brother?

Like him do I regard my faithfulness to duty as slavery, or do I see it as a labor of love?

When did I last encourage someone to return to the Father?

Did I take the time to accompany him or her on the way back?

69

COLLOQUY

Father, how much I harbor within me the unforgiving attitude of the elder brother. Like him I find it hard at times to forgive and forget. As I recall the countless times you have forgiven me, may this remembering change my stony heart into a loving, forgiving heart. Only your grace can effect this transformation within me. Thank you, Lord, for the miracle of your forgiving love.

16

The Other Nine

"On his journey to Jerusalem he passed along the borders of Samaria and Galilee. As he was entering a village, ten lepers met him. Keeping their distance, they raised their voices and said, 'Jesus, Master, have pity on us!' When he saw them, he responded, 'Go and show yourselves to the priests.' On their way there they were cured. One of them, realizing that he had been cured, came back praising God in a loud voice. He threw himself on his face at the feet of Jesus and spoke his praises. This man was a Samaritan.

"Jesus took the occasion to say, 'Were not all ten made whole? Where are the other nine? Was there no one to return and give thanks to God except this foreigner?' He said to the man, 'Stand up and go your way; your faith has been your salvation' " (Luke 17:11-19).

Walking with Jesus near the borders of Samaria on our journey to Jerusalem, we learn a much-needed lesson on gratitude. How much and how frequently we take the Lord's many-faceted love for granted!

These ten lepers were isolated from society. They were separated from their own people — family, friends, neighbors. They wanted very much to be healed.

As Jesus approached "they raised their voices and said, 'Jesus, Master, have pity on us!' " Jesus could not resist

71

their pleading. His heart was moved to pity. His tender love for the sick and the suffering overwhelmed him.

Jesus wanted to test the faith of the lepers. He did not heal them instantly. He waited to see if they trusted him. Therefore, he sent them off to the priests. At that time, the priests, who were both the civil and the religious authorities, had to pass judgment on whether or not a person was sufficiently healed to return to society. For this reason Jesus said: "Go and show yourselves to the priests."

Jesus might have had another reason for sending the lepers to the priests. He wanted to make the priests aware of the healing love with which he was touching all those who came to him. He also wanted the priests to recognize the divine power which enabled him to heal. Jesus hoped that this knowledge might awaken in the Jewish priests a nascent faith in him, and perhaps even influence them to accept him for what he was — the promised Messiah.

"On their way there they were cured." Imagine their joy and exultation. In their excitement and eagerness they must have rushed home to family and friends with the good news of their healing. In their preoccupation with themselves, they forgot Jesus and his tremendous healing love. They failed to thank him. Jesus was aware of this. He expected more from them and was disappointed.

> "Were not all ten made whole? Where are the other nine? Was there no one to return and give thanks to God except this foreigner?"

This man was a Samaritan. The Samaritans were considered heretics, yet this man was grateful. He realized the love and goodness of Jesus and came back to thank him.

Does this incident prick our conscience? Our loving Father is such a provident God. He has gifted us with life. He sustains and energizes us at every moment of the day. He supplies all the oxygen we need for some 25,000 respirations each day. Every heartbeat is his gift to us.

None of us has ever been threatened with starvation,

nor did we suffer from hunger for a protracted period. We enjoy the gift of sight to drink in the beauty of God's creation. We are blessed with the gift of hearing, enabling us to converse with others, to enjoy the sounds of music, the birds, wind, etc. Most of us are mobile and ambulatory. We can walk to and fro without much difficulty. God has given us family and friends who accept us and through whom he shares his love with us.

How many times Jesus has nourished us with himself in the Eucharist! How many times did Jesus say to us after absolving us: "Stand up and go your way: your faith has been your salvation!"

Reflection on this incident naturally leads us to ask ourselves where we stand in our relationship with Jesus — among the nine — or hopefully with the one.

REVIEW OF LIFE

Do I regularly, daily thank the Lord for his manifold gifts? Am I grateful for the many times I have been cleansed from the leprosy of sin?

After I receive sacramental absolution, do I take time to thank Jesus?

Do I spontaneously thank others for their many kindnesses to me?

COLLOQUY

Jesus, how often you say to me, "Go show yourself to the priest, that I may cleanse you from the leprosy of your sinfulness." Lord, I am not suffering the privation and isolation which the lepers endured; hence, the experiential awareness of your forgiving, healing love in the Sacrament of Reconciliation is not so apparent to me. With the help of your grace I want to join the one leper who returned to praise and thank you.

17

Where Do I Sit?

"He went on to address a parable to the guests, noticing how they were trying to get the places of honor at the table:

" 'When you are invited by someone to a wedding party, do not sit in the place of honor in case some greater dignitary has been invited. Then the host might come and say to you, "Make room for this man," and you would have to proceed shamefacedly to the lowest place. What you should do when you have been invited is go and sit in the lowest place, so that when your host approaches you he will say, "My friend, come up higher." This will win you the esteem of your fellow guests. For everyone who exalts himself shall be humbled and he who humbles himself shall be exalted' " (Luke 14:7-11).

Like the rest of us, the Jews were a proud lot. Their pride manifested itself in many ways. They were meticulous about the seating arrangement in the synagogue, at weddings, etc. No ordinary person would dare to occupy the place of some dignitary.

Jesus capitalized on this propensity to pride, to teach us a valuable lesson about pride and humility. When he noticed that they were trying to get the places of honor at the table, Jesus advised them to take the lowest place so that the host could say, "My friend, come up higher."

Jesus promised: "This will win you the esteem of your fellow guests." And the warning:

"Everyone who exalts himself shall be humbled and he who humbles himself shall be exalted."

Pride plagues the human race. Pride often originates in insecurity and the crying need for recognition and acceptance.

We feel threatened when someone questions our opinions or actions. We become defensive. We feel challenged by a harmless remark, often not intended for us at all.

Pride causes us to be easily offended by even innocent comments. If someone else is chosen instead of us for a particular honor or position we are disappointed and often filled with resentment, and even bitterness. We are inclined to retaliate.

Pride keeps us self-centered. We extol our own achievements, gifts, and talents. We are prone to talk endlessly about ourselves. We find it difficult to be grateful or to acknowledge the virtues and accomplishments of another.

There is a false kind of humility rooted in pride. Though we appear to deny or pass off our God-given gifts when we are complimented, in reality, we want to draw more attention to ourselves. This is humility with a hook. While we pretend not to possess these gifts, we hope that others will continue to compliment us and insist that we do possess fine qualities or have indeed accomplished great things.

Jesus understood these sinful tendencies in our broken human nature. He taught us humility by living humbly himself.

Humility is not weakness. Humility is the truth — the truth about God and what he does for us and the truth about ourselves that of ourselves we are nothing. It is only by cooperating with God's gifts and graces that we are able to achieve any measure of success.

Our Blessed Mother is an ideal example, a paragon of

humility. She admitted: "All ages to come shall call me blessed," but she also gave credit where it was due, to God alone. "God who is mighty has done great things for me, holy is his name" *(Luke 1:46ff).*

Jesus thanked and praised his Father for giving the humble, simple people the understanding of his truth.

"Father, Lord of heaven and earth, to you I offer praise; for what you have hidden from the learned and the clever you have revealed to the merest children" *(Matthew 11:25).* If there is seat-selection, which seat would I choose?

REVIEW OF LIFE

How do I accept compliments and thanks?

Am I easily hurt or disappointed when I am not recognized or honored in a gathering?

Am I over-sensitive to criticism?

When I am corrected, challenged or insulted, do I pout, withdraw or even, in my own mind, threaten to retaliate?

COLLOQUY

Lord Jesus, you bade me learn from you, because you are gentle and humble of heart. Help me to swallow my pride and recognize that all I am, all I have, and all I have accomplished is your gift to me. Teach me to pray with your Mother: "God who is mighty has done great things for me, holy is his name."

18

The Good Samaritan

On one occasion a teacher of Jewish religious law stood up to pose this problem to Jesus:

'' 'Teacher, what must I do to inherit everlasting life?' Jesus answered him: 'What is written in the law? How do you read it?' He replied: 'You shall love the Lord your God with all your heart, with all your soul, with all your strength, and with all your mind; and your neighbor as yourself.'

"Jesus said, 'You have answered correctly. Do this and you shall live.' But because he wished to justify himself he said to Jesus, 'And who is my neighbor?' Jesus replied: 'There was a man going down from Jerusalem to Jericho who fell prey to robbers. They stripped him, beat him, and then went off leaving him half-dead. A priest happened to be going down the same road; he saw him but continued on. Likewise there was a Levite who came the same way; he saw him and went on. But a Samaritan who was journeying along came on him and was moved to pity at the sight. He approached him and dressed his wounds, pouring in oil and wine. He then hoisted him on his own beast and brought him to an inn, where he cared for him. The next day he took out two silver pieces and gave them to the innkeeper with the request: ''Look after him, and if there is any further expense I will repay you on my way back." Which of these three, in your opinion, was neighbor to the man who fell in with the robbers?' The answer came, 'The one who treated him with compassion.' Jesus said to him, 'Then go and do the same' " *(Luke 10:25-37)*.

Jesus' teaching in the Gospel is always gentle, but persuasive. On occasion it is incisive and poignant. His teaching is direct and touches the receptive heart.

Contemplating the Good Samaritan parable can lead us to introspection and arouse a sense of neglect or of guilt within us. We easily become oblivious to our sins of omission.

"There was a man going down from Jerusalem to Jericho." This could have been a figurative expression. Jerusalem was considered the Holy City while Jericho was sin-city number one.

Jesus could also have meant this in the literal sense. The setting is ideal for the happenings in this story. The road to Jericho was a notoriously dangerous road. It was a steep, rocky, narrow road which twisted and turned through narrow canyons and around many rocky projections. It was infested with robbers and brigands who could conceal themselves in this rugged terrain.

Let us look at the person involved in this parable.

The Victim: This man was either foolhardy or ignorant. Rarely would anyone attempt to travel this road alone. They usually sought safety in numbers and travelled in convoys or caravans.

The Jewish Priest: "A priest happened to be going down the same road; he saw him but continued on." Perhaps the priest was on his way to the Temple to take his turn of duty in the ceremonies of the Temple worship. If he came in contact with a dead person, he would be rendered unclean for seven days according to the ritualistic law. These regulations meant more to him than the demands of love of neighbor. He did not want to get involved. "He saw him but continued on."

The Levite: "Likewise there was a Levite who came the same way; he saw him and went on." The Levite was a practical man in the eyes of the world. Bandits were in the habit of using decoys. One of their number would pretend to be a victim suffering along the road. When some unsuspecting traveller stopped to assist the apparently injured person, the other brigands would attack him and overpower him.

The Levite would take no chances. He was thinking of his own safety. This man desperately needed his help, but it was the man's own fault. Why should he, a Levite, be concerned about him?

Dwelling on the details of this parable invites an examination of conscience. Have we ever acted like the Jewish priest or the Levite?

In this story Jesus teaches valuable lessons. We are called to help people even when they brought troubles upon themselves, as this traveller had done. Secondly, every needy person in the world is our neighbor. Our vision must be as cosmic as the love of God is universal. Thirdly, our help must be practical, not merely a feeling of sorrow for the person. Love must be translated into action.

Jesus placed high priority on love of neighbor. After telling us that the first and greatest commandment was to love the Lord our God with our whole heart, soul and mind, Jesus is quick to add: "The second is like it; you shall love your neighbor as yourself" *(Matthew 22:39).*

On the night before he died Jesus reiterated with great emphasis the necessity of loving our neighbor.

"I give you a new commandment: Love one another. Such as my love has been for you, so must your love be for each other. This is how all will know you for my disciples: your love for one another" *(John 13:34-35).*

The first letter of John reads:

"The commandment we have from him is this: whoever loves God must also love his brother" *(I John 4:21).*

REVIEW OF LIFE

Have I consciously passed anyone by recently?

Do I feel pressed for time when someone needs my help?

Who is my neighbor?

Do I excuse myself from reaching out in love to some person because I feel he or she has brought on their own plight?

COLLOQUY

Jesus, how often I am too preoccupied with what I think are important matters to be concerned about those around me who are reaching out for some sign of loving care. Thank you for reminding me that loving concern must be a priority in my life. Help me to recognize you in every person who crosses my path today.

19

Golden Rule

"Treat others the way you would have them treat you: this sums up the law and the prophets" (Matthew 7:12).

In this one brief statement Jesus presents a life-long challenge to us. It will confront us every day of our earthly sojourn.

A proselyte once asked the famous teacher Rabbi Hillel to explain the whole law while he stood on one foot. Hillel responded:

"That which displeases you do not do to another. This is the whole Law; the rest is commentary."

Jesus went one step further. His pronouncement is more positive. He not only urges us not to do anything harmful or displeasing to another, but rather to do something good for another person. Jesus urges us not simply to avoid harming another person, but to show him or her loving care and concern.

Jesus not only taught us this brief mandate in his Sermon on the Mount, but he lived the Golden Rule throughout his whole earthly sojourn. This way of life is incorporated in the great commandment:

"You shall love your neighbor as yourself" (Matthew 22:39).

Jesus also went beyond the law to give us the rationale for this maxim. Jesus is present with and within every one of us in his resurrected life. Together with our brothers and sisters we form the Body of Christ — the People of God, his kingdom on earth. Jesus is the Head and we are the members. This means that whatever we do affects the whole Body for good or for evil.

Even our most private sin touches all the people of God — the whole Body. Conversely, when we seek reconciliation, or when we reach out in love to someone, God through us sanctifies all the members of the Body.

Paradoxically, this is both a frightening truth, yet a most consoling mystery, attested to by Jesus:

> "I assure you, as often as you did it for one of my least brothers, you did it for me" *(Matthew 25:40)*.

Jesus means this literally because he is dwelling in each one of us. Our Baptism incorporates us into the Body of Christ. We become the temples of the Holy Spirit. "You must know that your body is the temple of the Holy Spirit" *(I Corinthians 6:19)*.

On many different occasions Jesus promised that he would dwell with us, enlivening us, energizing us, loving us.

> "Anyone who loves me will be true to my word, and my Father will love him; we will come to him and make our dwelling place with him" *(John 14:23)*.

What privileged persons we are!

This certainly gives us ample reason to reflect on our own attitudes — our own actions and reactions to all the people we encounter.

St. Paul urges us to be aware of the presence of the risen Jesus in our family, our friends and neighbors as well as in our enemies. In his pastoral zeal he is continually reminding us to conduct ourselves accordingly.

"Out of love, place yourselves at one another's service. The whole law has found its fulfillment in this one saying: 'You shall love your neighbor as yourself.' If you go on biting and tearing one another to pieces, take care! You will end up in mutual destruction" *(Galatians 5:13-15)*.

And again:

"I plead with you, then . . . to live a life worthy of the calling you have received, with perfect humility, meekness, and patience, bearing with one another lovingly. Make every effort to preserve the unity which has the Spirit as its origin and peace as its binding force" *(Ephesians 4:1-3)*.

Let us linger with another fatherly bit of advice from St. Paul.

"Because you are God's chosen ones, holy and beloved, clothe yourselves with heartfelt mercy, with kindness, humility, meekness, and patience. Bear with one another; forgive whatever grievances you have against one another. Forgive as the Lord has forgiven you" *(Colossians 3:12-13)*.

St. Paul is focusing on the Golden Rule with some very practical ways of implementing it in our daily living.

REVIEW OF LIFE

How can I be more aware that Jesus is present in all my brothers and sisters?

How can I respect the dignity of each person as a temple of the Holy Spirit?

How can I make the Golden Rule the norm of my life?

Do I sincerely believe that what I do and say to another person, I am doing and saying to Jesus?

COLLOQUY

Lord Jesus, I am so sensitive to what others may say to me or about me, and to how they treat me; yet my own actions and attitudes toward others do not portray the same solicitude for them.

Keep me ever aware that what I do or say to others I am doing and saying to you, Lord.

20

Missing the Mark

"He said to them, 'When you pray, say: Father, hallowed be your name, your kingdom come. Give us each day our daily bread. Forgive us our sins for we too forgive all who do us wrong; and subject us not to the trial' " *(Luke 11:2-4)*.

Jesus effectively summarized the Christian attitudes which are essential for us if we are to deepen our relationship with our loving Father and eventually reach our final and full union with him.

Jesus included these conditions in the Lord's Prayer or the Our Father. This was a custom of his times. When a rabbi of his day taught his disciples, he often summarized his teaching into a prayer which his disciples committed to memory.

One of the petitions in the Lord's Prayer is:

"Forgive us our sins."

Sin is an unpopular word and many people have incorrect notions of sin. Many would agree that murder, adultery, blasphemy and thieving are sinful. If we have not fallen into these sins, we can thank God, but we ought not to conclude that we are not sinners because we are not guilty of these crimes. To live an ordinary respectable life, not to have ever been brought into court, nor ever to have been incarcerated, not to have incurred undue notoriety for misdeeds, does not mean that we are not sinners.

In the Scriptures we find a different idea of sin. The New Testament Greek uses five different words for sin. The most common word, translated literally, means "to miss the target." Sin is the failure to hit the mark. Sin is a failure to be what we might have been and what we could have been.

As we ponder this meaning, many of us will recognize the many opportunities and graces we have missed or abused. Often we may fail to reach out in love to others, or to enrich our relationship with our loving Father by spending more time in prayer. These are but a few of the ways we might have failed "to hit the target."

Another word for sin in the original language of the New Testament is the word "debt." Sin is then a failure to pay that which is due, a failure in duty.

All of us are indebted to so many people: parents, family, friends and a host of others. We owe them a debt of gratitude often not paid. Who of us would ever dare to claim that we have fulfilled all our duties toward God? I think the answer is obvious.

Have we thanked God sufficiently for the myriad blessings of each day? Have we given him the honor, reverence and respect we owe the transcendent God of heaven and earth? When have we last thanked God for every heartbeat, the gift of sight, our ability to walk — to mention only a few?

How often and sincerely we need to say: "Forgive us our sins."

As we pray the Lord's Prayer regularly, we are being reminded that the Lord is faithful to his promise to forgive us each time we contritely beg his forgiveness. The psalmist reassures us:

"The promises of the Lord are sure, like tried silver, freed from dross, sevenfold refined" (Psalm 12:7).

REVIEW OF LIFE

Do I recognize my many faults and failures and humbly present them to the Lord to ask his forgiveness?

Do I take time to review my day to ascertain whether or not I am on target?

Do I pray the Lord's Prayer slowly and reflectively, pausing and pondering each petition?

Do I say "Thank you" to God and to all who do so much for me in the course of each day?

COLLOQUY

Lord, Jesus, Redeemer and Savior of the world, you loved me so much that you were eager and willing to give up your life for my redemption. Please keep me on target. Create in me a grateful heart and continue to forgive me all my failures to hit the mark. Amen.

21

Forgive and Forget

"This is how you are to pray:

" 'Our Father in heaven, hallowed be your name, your kingdom come, your will be done on earth as it is in heaven. Give us today our daily bread, and forgive us the wrong we have done as we forgive those who wrong us. Subject us not to the trial but deliver us from the evil one' " *(Matthew 6:9ff)*.

Jesus taught that to become his disciples, we need a willingness to forgive those who have wronged us. To keep us ever mindful of this, Jesus incorporated it in the Lord's Prayer.

"Forgive us the wrong we have done as we forgive those who wrong us."

Verbalizing this petition is apt to prick our conscience. Experience attests how hard it is to forgive and forget. We ask God to forgive us even as we forgive those who wrong us.

When hurt, ridiculed, criticized, slandered or made to suffer some grave injustice, how difficult it is to say: "I forgive you."

Yet Jesus was insistent:

"If you forgive the faults of others, your heavenly Father will forgive you yours. If you do not forgive others, neither will your Father forgive you" *(Matthew 6:14f)*.

These words may cause concern and anxiety. We may have tried to forgive and forget, but in our own estimation have not succeeded. The hurts, wounds and scars may be too deep. Are we ourselves then not forgiven?

As we struggle with our efforts to forgive and forget, Jesus comes to our rescue. Jesus looks at our intentions and our will. If we truly desire and are striving to forgive others, Jesus is pleased. He knows our weakness. He knows that if we could forgive perfectly, he would have to endow us with special gifts. Of ourselves we cannot do so. In his infinite goodness, Jesus looks at our honest, sincere efforts.

Secondly, Jesus came into the world as our Redeemer and Healer. He wants to heal us of all our hurts. However, he cannot do so, unless we are open and receptive to his healing love. An oft-repeated prayer "Lord, heal me" makes us receptive to his healing power.

In the Sacrament of Penance, a special channel of healing, Jesus not only forgives our sins, but also heals us. When we need a healing, the frequent reception of this Sacrament will help us immensely.

Recall the meeting of Jesus with blind Bartimaeus, who called out, "Jesus, Son of David, have pity on me! . . ." Jesus asked him, "What do you want me to do for you?" "Rabboni, I want to see" *(Mark 10:46ff)*.

Our first impression is that it should have been quite obvious what Bartimaeus wanted. Nevertheless, Jesus wanted the blind man and the many others he healed to understand all the implications of living a different lifestyle after they were healed — to accept all that it implied.

Anyone who begged for a living knew that if he or she were healed, they would have to find another means of earning a livelihood.

Jesus did not, nor will he ever, force himself upon us. He waits for us. If he forgives us, and helps us to forgive others, it calls for changes in our attitudes and in our personal relationship with others.

If we want to nurse our hurts, pains and wounds, Jesus cannot heal us. But we can be certain that if we open ourselves with humility and sincerity to his healing power, he will heal us and help us to forgive and forget.

REVIEW OF LIFE

When I am hurt do I wallow in self-pity, or do I beg the Lord's healing?

Do I threaten to retaliate or to get even when I am hurt?

Do I receive the Sacrament of Reconciliation more frequently when I find it hard to forgive?

Do I pray for the person, or persons, who have wronged me?

COLLOQUY

Lord, let me sit with you on Calvary's hill. As I listen to all the scorn and ridicule being hurled at you and, in response, hear you not only ask the Father to forgive your enemies, but even excuse them, how then can I refuse to forgive those who have hurt me? Grant me this gift, Lord.

22

Please Excuse Me

"A man was giving a large dinner and he invited many. At dinner time he sent his servant to say to those invited, 'Come along, everything is ready now.' But they began to excuse themselves, one and all. The first one said to the servant, 'I have bought some land and must go out and inspect it. Please excuse me.' Another said, 'I have bought five yoke of oxen and I am going out to test them. Please excuse me.' A third said, 'I am newly married and so I cannot come.' The servant returning reported all this to his master. The master of the house grew angry at the account. He said to his servant, 'Go out quickly into the streets and alleys of the town and bring in the poor and the crippled, the blind and the lame.' The servant reported, after some time, 'Your orders have been carried out, my lord, and there is still room.' The master then said to the servant, 'Go out into the highways and along the hedgerows and force them to come in. I want my house to be full, but I tell you that not one of those invited shall taste a morsel of my dinner' " (Luke 14:16-24).

This parable speaks eloquently about our own reactions to Jesus' gracious invitation.

In the time of Jesus it was customary for a host to send out invitations to a dinner by way of a courier. The day of the dinner was set but not the exact time. In those days food preparation was more uncertain with no cooling or freezing units, nor any time-controlled stoves. For this reason, when dinner was nearly ready, the servants were sent out to summon guests who waited at home.

In this instance the guests were already invited to the dinner. They knew about the day and had not declined the invitation. However, when the servant arrived to announce that dinner was ready, the invited guests excused themselves for a variety of flimsy reasons.

"I have bought some land and must go out and inspect it."

"I have bought five yoke of oxen and I am going out to test them."

"I am newly married and so I cannot come."

With the foreknowledge of the dinner, some planning and foresight would have made the acceptance of the invitations possible, or a legitimate excuse could have been tendered in advance.

In this event and the circumstances surrounding it, we may see our own attitudes reflected in the excuses offered. When the Lord invites us, do we use our self-imposed busyness as an excuse for not spending more time in prayer, or praying more regularly?

We may use the same excuse for not celebrating the Eucharist, or receiving the other sacraments more frequently. The Lord may invite us to reach out in love to someone in need, or to radiate his loving concern to others. Do we respond eagerly and graciously?

Are we imaged in the first excuse of the man who bought some land and had to go out to inspect it? The person who excused himself because he had bought five yoke of oxen and wanted to go out and test them was looking forward to a pleasant time and some recreation. He was not detained by some sort of emergency. He was merely "going out to test them."

Are there occasions when our ease and comfort, our

recreation and pleasure come first? It may be our favorite television program or our cherished recreation. Have we ever heard ourselves rationalizing that our relaxation comes first; and that tomorrow we can respond to the Lord's prompting?

The newly married man's excuse manifests a heart unwilling to listen to the Lord's request. On one occasion Jesus said:

> "Whoever loves father or mother, son or daughter, more than me is not worthy of me" *(Matthew 10:37)*.

> "If anyone comes to me without turning his back on his father and mother, his wife and his children, his brothers and sisters, indeed his very self, he cannot be my follower" *(Luke 14:26)*.

Jesus is in no way implying that a person should not love his family, but he is speaking about priorities. After all, Jesus instituted the Sacrament of marriage and were it not for the Lord's boundless love for us, there could be no love between husband and wife.

In this case the excuse was not valid since the dinner would take only a short time. The invitation was compatible with the man's marital status. In fact, his wife might have been happy to have her husband out of the house for a brief period especially since she did not have to prepare a meal for him. In short, it was a fabricated excuse.

Again we may find ourselves using rationalizations to excuse ourselves and to do only what we want to do.

Listen attentively as Jesus says to us: "Come along, everything is ready now."

REVIEW OF LIFE

When do I consider myself too busy to respond to the Lord's invitation?

Do I take time to rest in a listening posture to hear what the Lord is saying to me?

Do I pause throughout the day to ascertain if I am on the Lord's wavelength?

Do my rationalizations and self-centeredness keep me on the defensive, when the Lord is calling me to do his will?

PRAYER

Lord Jesus, please grant me the grace to recognize your call, the courage to die to self, the strength to rise above my selfishness and the generosity to respond to your call at all times. May I experience the peace and joy of knowing that I am doing what you wish me to do, and experience the bliss of my eternal union with you. Amen.

Redeeming
Love

23

Through the Gate to the Cross

" 'Truly I assure you: Whoever does not enter the sheepfold through the gate but climbs in some other way is a thief and a marauder. The one who enters through the gate is shepherd of the sheep; the keeper opens the gate for him. The sheep hear his voice as he calls his own by name and leads them out. When he has brought out (all) those that are his, he walks in front of them, and the sheep follow him because they recognize his voice. They will not follow a stranger; such a one they will flee, because they do not recognize a stranger's voice.'

"Even though Jesus used this figure with them, they did not grasp what he was trying to tell them. He therefore said (to them again):

" 'My solemn word is this: I am the sheepgate. All who came before me were thieves and marauders whom the sheep did not heed. I am the gate. Whoever enters through me will be safe. He will go in and out, and find pasture. The thief comes only to steal and slaughter and destroy. I came that they might have life and have it to the full. I am the good shepherd; the good shepherd lays down his life for the sheep. The hired hand — who is no shepherd nor owner of the sheep — catches sight of the wolf coming and runs away, leaving the sheep to be snatched and scattered by the wolf. That is because he works for pay; he has no concern for the sheep. I am the good shepherd. I know my sheep and my sheep know me in the same way that the Father knows me and I know the Father; for these sheep I will give my life. I have other sheep that do not belong to this fold. I must lead them, too, and they shall hear my voice. There shall be one flock then, one shepherd. The Father loves me for this: that I lay down my life to take it up again. No one takes it from me; I lay it down freely. I have power to lay it down, and I have power to take it up again. This command I received from my Father" *(John 10:1-18)*.

The image of the shepherd is used extensively in Sacred Scripture. A shepherd feeds his sheep, watches over them and protects them. He cares for their every need. He loves them.

Speaking through his prophet, the Lord describes himself as the Good Shepherd. When the human shepherds to whom he entrusts his people fail, the Lord himself cares for his sheep.

"I myself will look after and tend my sheep. As a shepherd tends his flock when he finds himself among his scattered sheep, so will I tend my sheep" *(Ezekiel 34:11-12)*.

The Father describes his healing, redeeming love:

"I myself will pasture my sheep; I myself will give them rest, says the Lord God. The lost I will seek out, the strayed I will bring back, the injured I will bind up, the sick I will heal . . . shepherding them rightly" *(Ezekiel 34:15-16)*.

Tenderly the Father reveals his loving care for all who are wounded and broken because of sinfulness.

It is not surprising, then, to find in the New Testament that Jesus refers to himself as the Good Shepherd, who cares for us and provides for us. He loves us, his sheep, so much that he willingly lays down his life for us:

"I am the good shepherd; the good shepherd lays down his life for the sheep."

Jesus laid down his life in order to redeem us and to give us his divine life. He wants to make certain we understand that he gave his life freely because he loves us and that he was not forced to do so:

"The Father loves me for this: that I lay down my life to take it up again. No one takes it from me; I lay it down freely. I have the power to lay it down, and I have the power to take it up again."

Jesus gave himself in order to redeem us. His redemptive act made our broken, fallen human nature capable of receiving his divine life. By investing us with his divine life he reestablishes our union with the Godhead, tragically lost in the fall of our first parents.

"I came that they might have life and have it to the full."

This redemptive sharing of his life is not some vague or distant gift that may or may not touch us personally and individually. Redemption is the universal gift to the world, it is true, but it is also very personal. Jesus personalized his redeeming love in the Sacrament of Penance.

In this Sacrament we encounter the Person of Jesus, who pours out his forgiving, healing, redeeming love upon us and fills us with his divine life. Jesus is universal Lord, but he is also the Lord of each one of us personally and individually. In this sacramental rite Jesus meets the strayed, binds up the wounds of the injured, heals the sick and sinful.

If we hear and recognize the voice of the Good Shepherd calling us to repentance, if we respond to him as docile sheep, he will protect and nourish us. For us were meant his words: "For these sheep I will give my life."

REVIEW OF LIFE

What did Jesus mean when he promised to give me life to the full?

How do I listen to the voice of the Shepherd?

As the Good Shepherd, Jesus knows me personally. How do I respond to his protective, providing, caring love?

What is my response to Jesus' words: "There is no greater love than this: to lay down one's life for one's friends"?

COLLOQUY

Jesus, you are the Good Shepherd who gives your life for your sheep. Keep me attuned to your voice as you call me by name and lead me on your way of life. Give me a listening, docile heart to respond generously to your shepherding love. Please continue to protect, nourish and love me, so that I may have your life and have it to the full.

24

Never Alone

"Then Jesus went with them to a place called Gethsemani. He said to his disciples, 'Stay here while I go over there and pray.' He took along Peter and Zebedee's two sons, and began to experience sorrow and distress. Then he said to them, 'My heart is nearly broken with sorrow. Remain here and stay awake with me.' He advanced a little and fell prostrate in prayer. 'My Father, if it is possible, let this cup pass me by. Still, let it be as you would have it, not as I.' When he returned to his disciples, he found them asleep. He said to Peter, 'So you could not stay awake with me for even an hour? Be on guard, and pray that you may not undergo the test. The spirit is willing but nature is weak.' Withdrawing a second time he began to pray: 'My Father, if this cannot pass me by without my drinking it, your will be done!' Once more, on his return, he found them asleep; they could not keep their eyes open. He left them again, withdrew somewhat, and began to pray a third time, saying the same words as before. Finally he returned to his disciples and said to them: 'Sleep on now. Enjoy your rest! The hour is on us when the Son of Man is to be handed over to the power of evil men. Get up! Let us be on our way! See, my betrayer is here' " (Matthew 26:36-46).

During his agony in the Garden of Gethsemane, Jesus begged his disciples for their comforting presence and their prayer support to make this the greatest of all human decisions. He did not want to fight the battle alone.

He brought his disciples with him to the Mount of Olives and left some at the entrance of the Garden. He took his special prayer-team, Peter and Zebedee's two sons, with him into the inner Garden.

"My heart is nearly broken with sorrow. Remain here and stay awake with me."

When he returned and found them asleep:

"So you could not stay awake with me for even an hour? Be on your guard, and pray that you may not undergo the test."

St. Luke writes:

"In his anguish he prayed with all the greater intensity. . . . Then he rose from prayer and came to his disciples, only to find them asleep, exhausted with grief" (Luke 22:44-45).

When he needed his disciples the most, they went to sleep. Did they lack concern for him? Were they too preoccupied with self, feeling that they needed their rest? We do not know. All that we do know is that Jesus did not receive from them the encouragement and support he needed in this his hour.

Jesus calls us to prayer. There are occasions when we must endure a little agony, be it some anxiety or pain, some cross or disappointment, some problem or burden, some moments of discouragement.

Jesus recognizes that of ourselves, we are not able to accept the "cup." Our human nature may rebel. We may question God's loving providence. We may find the cross too cumbersome. We may even feel bitterness and resentment.

In such moments we may seek the consoling comfort of others who only augment our self-pity. We may seek help from those who cannot offer it. That is why Jesus showed us by his own example that prayer, and prayer alone, can help us.

When he bids us come to him for refreshment, he is inviting us to come to him in prayer. He reminds us that only after he spent time alone in prayer was he able to say: "Still, let it be as you would have it, not as I."

Jesus invites us to be with him in prayer because his Body, the People of God, our brothers and sisters, need our comfort and consolation. They need our prayerful and loving support. They are crying out to us.

If we neglect to reach out in prayerful support and loving concern for others who are facing grave trials and suffering, Jesus may chide us for our culpable omission with: "So you could not stay awake with me for even an hour?"

When a cross comes our way or when we are in agony, Jesus' advice is clear: "Wake up, and pray that you may not be subjected to the trial" *(Luke 22:46).*

REVIEW OF LIFE

How much time do I spend each day visiting with Jesus in prayer?

Does Jesus ever have to say to me: "Could you not stay awake with me for even an hour?"

In times of difficulty do I go immediately to Jesus in prayer, or do I seek consolation and advice from others first?

Do I pray for the discouraged, the burdened, the sick, the suffering, and for those who have strayed from the path of peace?

COLLOQUY

Jesus, what a powerful example you gave me as you were confronted with your ministry of suffering. When your agony became unbearable, you prayed "with all the greater intensity." Only in prayer were you able to submit willingly to your Father and say "not my will but yours be done." In facing my daily problems I often turn first to others for help and consolation rather than to you. Create in me a submissive spirit to embrace the Father's will as a loving response to the outpouring of his loving concern for me.

25

Heaven Stolen by an Expert

"One of the criminals hanging in crucifixion blasphemed him: 'Aren't you the Messiah? Then save yourself and us.' But the other one rebuked him: 'Have you no fear of God, seeing you are under the same sentence? We deserve it, after all. We are only paying the price for what we've done, but this man has done nothing wrong.' He then said, 'Jesus, remember me when you enter upon your reign.' And Jesus replied, 'I assure you: this day you will be with me in paradise' " *(Luke 23:39-43)*.

Jesus knew the hearts of all who came to him. As two criminals and Jesus hung on their deathbed of the cross, one of them rebuked his fellow criminal, who was blaspheming Jesus. The first man was truly contrite. He was acknowledging and admitting his guilt. He also recognized the mercy of the Lord. With sorrow he turned to Jesus and pleaded: "Jesus, remember me when you enter upon your reign."

Such a plea melted Jesus' heart. He said: "This day you will be with me in paradise." Jesus permitted the thief to steal heaven.

Even though Jesus was suffering the agonizing and suffocating pain of crucifixion, he was not thinking about himself. He had come to save and to redeem. During the closing hours of his earthly life, Jesus had reached out to so many, but they would not accept his loving forgiveness.

Jesus is in his glory now, but his glory consists in continuing his redemptive work on earth. He is patiently waiting for our repentance. He waits for us to ask his forgiveness and healing so that he can release the avalanche of his compassionate love upon us. He waits to flood our hearts with the peace and joy this world cannot give.

If there is some fear or hesitation, if we feel undeserving of his forgiveness, if we fear we might fall back into the same sin, listen to his encouraging words: "I love you just as you are. I don't care what you have done; I love you anyway."

God wants a sinner to be converted and live.

REVIEW OF LIFE

Am I aware that the Lord is waiting?

When I fail him in great or small ways, do I humbly go to him, realizing my need of his healing and forgiveness?

Like the Good Thief, do I admit my faults and failures?

Do I, like the other criminal, blame God for some of my misfortune?

COLLOQUY

Jesus, my Savior and Redeemer, you told us that you do not wish the death of a sinner, but that he be converted and live. When the enormity of my sinfulness wells up before me, I sometimes hesitate to ask your forgiveness. However, as I contemplate your gentle and gracious dealing with the Good Thief, I find much hope and encouragement, knowing that your compassionate mercy embraces me also. Jesus, as I approach the end of my earthly sojourn, please let me steal heaven also.

26

The Mystery of Love

"Father, forgive them; they do not know what they
are doing" *(Luke 23:34)*.

In pain and suffering, especially if that suffering is unjustly imposed, a person proves his true character. His
mettle is tested. He reveals much about his personality.

Triumphantly Jesus came through the test. No one suffered more inhumanly and more unjustly than did Jesus.
Throughout his dreadful passion and death, Jesus never ut-
tered a word of self-pity nor did he condemn or threaten.

On the contrary, Jesus prayed for his enemies and ex-
ecutioners: "Father, forgive them."

Even more, Jesus excused them before his Father.
"They do not know what they are doing."

Jesus still prays for us and excuses us before the Father.
Listen to the derision, the insults, the mockery, the
blasphemy being hurled at Jesus. Our sinfulness helped
nail him to the cross. We are included in his prayer.

"Jesus Christ is the same yesterday, today, and
forever" *(Hebrews 13:8)*.

Jesus still prays for us and still excuses us before the
Father.

Jesus knows how prone we are to be thoughtless, self-
centered, proud, impatient and judgmental, to mention
only a few of our faults. We find ourselves in good company. St. Paul lamented the same weakness:

"I cannot even understand my own actions. I do not do what I want to do but what I hate. . . . The desire to do right is there but not the power. . . . What a wretched man I am!" *(Romans 7:15ff).*

Paul asks: "Who can free me from this body under the power of death?" Then he remembers: "All praise to God, through Jesus Christ our Lord!"

How often we do the things we do not want to do! How weak we are!

Jesus foresees our good intentions and our brokenness: "Father, forgive them; they do not know what they are doing."

Discouragement is one of the strongest temptations which the devil can hurl into our path. He knows that if we become discouraged, we are simply not going to try. We will give up too easily.

Jesus sees not so much any particular sin or failing of ours, but primarily our honest desires. Do we want to love him enough to serve him faithfully? If this is our fundamental option, Jesus is pleased.

If through human weakness we momentarily veer off the target, Jesus understands. When we come to him in humility and sorrow, he excuses us: "They do not know what they are doing."

Jesus, excusing us before the Father, does not give us a license to sin. On the contrary, love wants to please the beloved as much as possible. We may think of sin only as a violation of a law. Disregarding or breaking a law may well be sinful, but the real malice of sin is the refusal to accede to the will of the lawgiver. In other words, obeying the will of another is an expression of our love for that person.

If we love God, we want to do what God wants of us. In this we manifest our love for him. Furthermore, anything God asks of us is for our own welfare.

In his final instruction, Jesus teaches us how to love:

107

"You will live in my love if you keep my commandments, even as I have kept my Father's commandments, and live in his love" *(John 15:10)*.

A loving heart will find it very difficult to sin. Sin is a refusal to love. Hearing Jesus pleading: "Father, forgive them: they do not know what they are doing," can we refuse to love?

REVIEW OF LIFE

As I ponder Jesus' words "Father, forgive them," what sentiments well up in my heart?

Does the consuming desire of Jesus to forgive me make it harder for me to sin, or do I abuse it as a license to sin knowing that I will be forgiven?

Do I take time to sit in spirit beneath the cross on Calvary to listen to all the infamy leveled at Jesus, knowing that my own sins contributed to his degradation?

When I hear Jesus begging for forgiveness for me, do I find it easier to forgive others?

COLLOQUY

Jesus, I sit astonished as I hear you begging forgiveness in your dying moment for all of us who crucified you. What a mystery is your love! I hear your prayer reechoed by your first martyr, Stephen: "Lord, do not hold this sin against them." Grant me the grace to pray for anyone who has wronged or hurt me as you prayed: "Father, forgive them; they do not know what they are doing."

108

No Room
for Fear

27

Fear Is Useless

"It is in Christ and through his blood that we have been redeemed and our sins forgiven, so immeasurably generous is God's favor to us. God has given us the wisdom to understand fully the mystery, the plan he was pleased to decree in Christ, to be carried out in the fullness of time: namely, to bring all things in the heavens and on earth into one under Christ's headship" *(Ephesians 1:7-10)*.

We have all experienced tension and anxiety, the embarrassment and guilt of having offended others, and the strained relationship existing between ourselves and them. The relationship may seem totally fragmented.

We regret our action and are ashamed of our conduct. We would like to restore our friendship, but are fearful. We are uncertain how the other person would accept us, if we tried to make amends or ask for forgiveness. We are afraid to risk rejection.

If the offended person takes the initiative and accepts us as we are with all our weaknesses, and wants to continue our friendship, we are overjoyed and delighted. Such graciousness enriches our friendship and causes it to grow and mature.

In another area of our life a similar situation exists, but with an eternal dimension. If we have involuntarily, or even deliberately, sinned against God, we experience the same conflicting reactions usually accompanied by a fear of punishment either temporal or eternal — either here or hereafter.

Our fear is groundless. Our redeeming Lord assures us of his eagerness to forgive and heal us, if we are disposed and receptive to his forgiving love.

St. Paul reminds us "how immeasurably generous is God's favor to us" for "it is in Christ and through his blood that we have been redeemed and our sins forgiven." Speaking through the prophet, our compassionate Father urges us:

> "Put away your misdeeds from before my eyes; cease doing evil; learn to do good. Make justice your aim: redress the wronged. . . ."

When we respond to his invitation the Father assures us:

> "Though your sins be like scarlet, they may become white as snow; though they be crimson red, they may become white as wool" *(Isaiah 1:16-18).*

If our anxiety and fear of not being forgiven persists, our loving Father continues:

> "Fear not, I have redeemed you; I have called you by name: you are mine" *(Isaiah 43:1).*

Repeatedly Jesus reassures us:

> "Fear is useless. What is needed is trust" *(Mark 5:36).*

> "I have not come to invite the self-righteous to a change of heart, but sinners" *(Luke 5:32).*

To our joy of being forgiven the "Father of mercies" also adds an enriched relationship with him.

We can unite our thanks with St. Paul:

"Praised be God, the Father of our Lord Jesus Christ, the Father of mercies, and the God of all consolation! He comforts us in all our afflictions and thus enables us to comfort those who are in trouble, with the same consolation we have received from him" (II Corinthians 1:3-4).

Once we have experienced such a consoling love and all the joy which its power brings us, we can certainly "comfort those who are in trouble with the same consolation we have received from him."

One of the ways of bringing this consolation to others is by inviting, or even bringing them to meet the "Father of mercies and the God of all consolation" in the Sacrament of Penance.

"Remember this: the person who brings a sinner back from his way will save his soul from death and cancel a multitude of sins" (James 5:20).

REVIEW OF LIFE

Do I distinguish between a reverential fear of God and a groundless worry or anxiety?

In a strained relationship do I depend on the other person to take the initiative for reconciliation, or do I take the first steps in Christian love?

Am I really convinced that the Lord wants to forgive me more than I could want it myself?

Do I love God enough to overcome any lack of trust in him?

COLLOQUY

O Father of mercies and God of all consolation, how comforting is your promise that if my sins be like scarlet, they will become white as snow. I am over-whelmed at your continuing compassion.

Let me share the peace and joy, the tranquility and serenity you have given me with at least one other person who has not experienced the consolation of your forgiveness. Inspire and guide me in bringing a strayed sheep back to you, my loving Shepherd.

28

Unworthiness Syndrome

"As Jesus entered Capernaum, a centurion approached him with this request: 'Sir, my serving boy is at home in bed paralyzed, suffering painfully.' He said to him, 'I will come and cure him.' 'Sir,' the centurion said in reply, 'I am not worthy to have you under my roof. Just give an order and my boy will get better. I am a man under authority myself and I have troops assigned to me. If I give one man the order, "Dismissed," off he goes. If I say to another, "Come here," he comes. If I tell my slave, "Do this," he does it.'

"Jesus showed amazement on hearing this and remarked to his followers, 'I assure you, I have never found this much faith in Israel. Mark what I say! Many will come from the east and the west and will find a place at the banquet in the kingdom of God with Abraham, Isaac, and Jacob, while the natural heirs of the kingdom will be driven out into the dark. Wailing will be heard there, and the grinding of teeth.' To the centurion Jesus said, 'Go home. It shall be done because you trusted.' That very moment the boy got better" (Matthew 8:5-13).

When we reflect upon our own waywardness, especially our repeated falls into the same sin, we wonder if God will continue to forgive us again and again. We make efforts to overcome a certain failing, only to fail again. We experience doubts or even grave fear of not being forgiven. We are filled with a sense of unworthiness, even discouragement.

In the Gospel Jesus reveals his attitude toward this unworthiness syndrome. When a Roman centurion asked Jesus to heal his serving boy, Jesus volunteered to go down to his house and heal the sick boy. The officer had great faith in Jesus and trusted that he could heal even at a distance; hence no need for him to go that extra distance. Notice the humility of the centurion as he replied: "I am not worthy to have you under my roof."

Jesus was not concerned about the man's worthiness or unworthiness, but was moved by the humble dispositions of the centurion's heart. It took great humility for a Roman officer to approach a Jew for a favor. Secondly, the official was not asking for anything for himself, but for a healing for his "serving boy." This manifested his great concern for his paralyzed servant. Slaves could be bought cheaply and this boy could easily be replaced, but the centurion's empathy dominated his pride.

Above all, Jesus was pleased with the man's faith. He did not go to the Roman officer's home. This could cause the official some embarrassment. He simply announced: "Go home. It shall be done because you trusted." That very moment the boy got better.

This humble attitude of the Roman centurion has been immortalized in the Eucharistic Liturgy, as we pray before Holy Communion: "Lord, I am not worthy to receive you; but only say the word and I shall be healed."

Another Gospel episode reveals Peter's sense of unworthiness and Jesus' reaction to it. Peter was an expert fisherman with all the skills of the trade. When Jesus advised Peter: "Put out into deep water and lower your nets for a catch," he objected: "Master, we have been hard at it all night long and have caught nothing; but if you say so, I will lower the nets" *(Luke 5:4-11)*.

This was a blow to Peter's pride, but in his weak, wavering faith he complied. "Upon doing this they caught such a great number of fish that their nets were at the breaking point." Peter recognized the divine intervention and saw his own unworthiness in the presence of Jesus and his divine power. "Simon Peter fell at the knees of Jesus saying, 'Leave me, Lord. I am a sinful man.'"

Jesus saw not Simon Peter's unworthiness, but his great potential and his humility. Instead of leaving him as Peter requested, Jesus called him to a greater vocation. "Do not be afraid. From now on you will be catching men."

Jesus' contemplative heart sees beneath the superficial. He knows and understands our unworthiness, but he also is aware of our desire to lead a life free from sin. Jesus is always eager and ready to forgive.

To personalize his forgiveness he instituted the Sacrament of Penance as the means whereby he could shower his forgiving, healing, redeeming love upon us.

When Napoleon was not receiving the sacraments he excused himself on the plea that he was not worthy. He engaged in discussions with learned theologians who tried to convince him to no avail.

One day a simple country pastor responded to Napoleon's excuse with: "Yes, Sire, you are right. You are not worthy, but you need the sacraments." This simple reply shattered the great ruler's arguments.

Jesus does not take into consideration our unworthiness, but rather the dispositions of our heart. If we honestly acknowledge our sinfulness and humbly come to Jesus seeking his forgiveness, his overwhelming love cleanses and heals us. Jesus really meant it when he said: "Come to me, all you who are weary and find life burdensome, and I will refresh you" (Matthew 11:28).

REVIEW OF LIFE

Do I discover some of Napoleon's attitude in myself?

Does my feeling of unworthiness keep me from asking God's forgiveness?

Do I fear that I am not worthy to be forgiven?

If I doubt my sorrow for sin, or my resoluteness to avoid a particular sin, what am I to do?

How great is my trust in Jesus' promise to forgive, heal and redeem me?

COLLOQUY

Jesus, my Savior and Redeemer, my sense of unworthiness stems from my pride which blinds me to your merciful, compassionate love. You are eager to forgive my waywardness. Help me to keep my focus riveted on you as I place all my sinfulness into the crucible of your consuming love.

29

Love — A Super-Power

"Beloved, let us love one another because love is of God; everyone who loves is begotten of God and has knowledge of God. The man without love has known nothing of God, for God is love. God's love was revealed in our midst in this way: he sent his only Son to the world that we might have life through him. Love, then, consists in this: not that we have loved God, but that he has loved us and has sent his Son as an offering for our sins. Beloved, if God has loved us so, we must have the same love for one another" (I John 4:7-11).

Jesus came to redeem and heal us that we might live in peace and harmony with one another. To accept one another lovingly we need to be healed of our self-centeredness, our sensitivity, our wounded pride, our short-sightedness, our spirit of retaliation and numerous other weaknesses which scar our personality.

We are all members of the Body of Christ, the People of God. What we do as individuals affects the whole Body. If we sin, the whole Body is poorer because of our lack of love. On the other hand, each time we strive to die to self and put on the new man, which is Jesus, we bring blessings to the whole people of God.

Jesus understands our humanness, our brokenness, and how difficult it is for us to accept others just as they are. He commands us to love our neighbors as ourselves, but he also knows we will fail from time to time. For this reason he continues to forgive, heal and redeem us so that we can live happily and peacefully as members of his Body.

When Jesus directed us to love one another, he called it a new commandment. He also said that our love for one another would give witness to the world of our discipleship.

"I give you a new commandment: Love one another. Such as my love has been for you, so must your love be for each other. This is how all will know you for my disciples: your love for one another" (John 13:34-35).

St. Paul exhorts and admonishes us to live this love:

"Because you are God's chosen ones, holy and beloved, clothe yourselves with heartfelt mercy, with kindness, humility, meekness, and patience. . . . Forgive as the Lord has forgiven you. Over all these virtues put on love, which binds the rest together and makes them perfect. Christ's peace must reign in your hearts, since as members of the one body you have been called to that peace. Dedicate yourselves to thankfulness. Let the word of Christ, rich as it is, dwell in you" (Colossians 3:12-16).

What a challenge for us at every moment of every day! We would do well to reflect word by word or phrase by phrase on Paul's directives. This will reveal the depth of our own Christian commitment.

We pray at Mass:

"Grant that we, who are nourished by his body and blood, may be filled with his Holy Spirit and become one body, one spirit in Christ" (III Eucharistic Prayer).

"May all of us who share in the body and blood of Christ be brought together in unity by the Holy Spirit" (II Eucharistic Prayer).

REVIEW OF LIFE

Do I consistently ask the Lord to heal me when someone is annoying me?

Do I frequently recall that the Lord has always and without hesitation forgiven me and that I should forgive others in the same way?

Since others bear with me and my idiosyncrasies, how do I bear with others as they are?

What is my awareness and reaction to the fact that all that I do for good or evil affects the whole Body of Christ and that I do have an obligation to all the people of God?

PRAYER

"May God, the source of all patience and encouragement, enable you to live in perfect harmony with one another according to the spirit of Christ Jesus, so that with one heart and voice you may glorify God, the Father of our Lord Jesus Christ" (Romans 15:5-6).

Called to Live

30

In His Footprints

''The next day John was there again with two of his
disciples. As he watched Jesus walk by he said,
'Look! There is the Lamb of God!' The two disciples
heard what he said, and followed Jesus. When
Jesus turned around and noticed them following
him, he asked them, 'What are you looking for?'
They said to him, 'Rabbi (which means Teacher),
where do you stay?' 'Come and see,' he answered.
So they went to see where he was lodged, and
stayed with him that day. (It was about four in the
afternoon.)'' *(John 1:35-39)*.

After Jesus was baptized in the river Jordan, two of the
disciples of John the Baptizer followed him as he walked
away. When Jesus turned to them and asked: ''What are
you looking for?'' the disciples were startled momentarily
but managed to ask: ''Rabbi, where do you stay?''

Jesus' response was brief, but implied much more than
these few words seem to indicate. Jesus simply said:
''Come and see.'' He was not merely inviting them to come
and see in what kind of shelter he was staying, but rather
to come and see for themselves who he was, what he was
teaching, and what kind of life-style he was advocating.

Jesus was inviting them to come and stay with him, to
listen to him, to pray with him, to imitate his life-style.
Like the other masters of his day, Jesus did not teach his
disciples so much by imparting information to them ver-

bally; rather they learned by observation and by striving to live as he did.

Jesus is inviting us to "come and see," to become his disciples. Baptism was our formal initiation into discipleship. When we became members of the family of God, we were asked to make our commitment to the way of life which Jesus laid down for us. That commitment is an ongoing commitment. Each day we are asked to live out our baptismal commitment more fully.

In order to understand all the implications of our commitment, Jesus is inviting us to rest in his presence. He wants us to put ourselves totally at his disposal, to open our minds and hearts to what he is striving to impart to us. He is asking us to listen to his word and to permit that word to penetrate our whole being, to let it mold and transform us.

We are called to be Christians — disciples of Jesus. Of the millions of people in the world, Jesus is inviting us personally and individually to be his followers. What a privilege!

Christians are to have the same mind and heart that Jesus had. Our wills must be in tune with the will of our loving Father. "Your attitude must be that of Christ" (Philippians 2:5). Paul continues:

> "Acquire a fresh, spiritual way of thinking. You must put on that new man created in God's image, whose justice and holiness are born of truth" (Ephesians 4:23-24).

It is easy to procrastinate, hoping someday to follow the Lord more closely; so easy to become so engrossed in the secular pursuits of the world that the way of life Jesus laid down for a Christian can slip far down the list of our priorities.

REVIEW OF LIFE

Do I "come and see" by spending time each day in the prayer of listening?

Do I observe Jesus' ministry in the Gospel, recognizing his loving concern for others?

Do I rest in the sunshine of Jesus' presence and strive to know him as a person, rather than simply to know more about him?

How is my role as a disciple radiating the Lord's love and joy?

PRAYER

"Lord Jesus, I see your footprints all about me beckoning me to follow you more closely by accepting a little rebuff, by showing loving concern, by listening to a tale of woe, by pausing to say thank you to my provident Father. Jesus, please keep your strides short that I may persevere in my following you. Amen."

31

An RSVP Invitation

"Afterward he went out and saw a tax collector named Levi sitting at his customs post. He said to him, 'Follow me.' Leaving everything behind, Levi stood up and became his follower. After that Levi gave a great reception for Jesus in his house, in which he was joined by a large crowd of tax collectors and others at dinner. The Pharisees and the scribes of their party said to his disciples, 'Why do you eat and drink with tax collectors and non-observers of the law?' Jesus said to them, 'The healthy do not need a doctor; sick people do. I have not come to invite the self-righteous to a change of heart, but sinners' " (Luke 5:27-32).

In the ministry of Jesus, we discover a recurrent invitation. As Jesus invited Matthew and the other disciples to follow him, he invites us personally to become his disciples. We may not be able to leave everything as Matthew did, nor does Jesus intend such a total withdrawal for everyone.

Jesus is inviting us to follow him by being lovingly concerned about family and friends and others. Jesus wants us to die to self and be filled with his divine life and love.

Jesus invites us to become his disciples, following in his footsteps so closely that we can be identified with him.

Jesus' invitation carries with it an RSVP. We need to assess our lives to discover whether we are responding graciously and generously, or is our response half-hearted, or have we even ignored his invitation?

When Jesus suggested to the rich man that he should sell his goods and give to the poor, "the man's face fell. He went away sad." Jesus must have been disappointed, for the evangelist says: "Jesus looked at him with love" (Mark 10:17ff).

On another occasion, when Jesus promised his greatest gift — the gift of himself in the Eucharist, it was too much for some of his followers.

"From this time on, many of his disciples broke away and would not remain in his company any longer" (John 6:66).

Jesus invites us to be his disciples because he loves us and wants to be closely associated with us. Love always wants to be close to the beloved, to share life with the person loved. Jesus wants us to be close to him. In fact, he loves us so much he lives with us and within us and makes us the temples of the Holy Spirit.

He wants us to live in peace and harmony during our sojourn on earth. Jesus knows that his way of life is the only source of genuine happiness. He begs us to come to him so that we may learn it. This will assure us of our union with him for all eternity. This is what Jesus desires for each one of us: "No one who comes will I ever reject" (John 6:37). Jesus continues:

"Indeed, this is the will of my Father, that everyone who looks upon the Son and believes in him shall have eternal life. Him I will raise up on the last day" (John 6:40).

Living a good Christian life is much more than avoiding sin. It means following the life-style of Jesus and permitting him to transform us into reflecting his love, peace and joy wherever we go.

We need to appraise our lives honestly and sincerely to

ascertain if we have given our RSVP to Jesus wholeheartedly. Sometimes it is more difficult for us to be aware of our sins of omission than the sins of commission. Our failure to respond to his invitation could be sinful neglect. To say the least, it is highly impolite not to accept a special invitation. We need to review our life periodically to ascertain how we are really listening to Jesus' call and responding to it.

REVIEW OF LIFE

How attentively do I listen to Jesus' invitation? Am I fearful that he will ask more than I am willing to give?

Do I renew regularly, even daily, my response to Jesus' invitation to follow him more closely?

Do I strive to die to self in little ways throughout the day?

Do I recognize the privilege of being called to be a disciple, hearing Jesus say to me: "It was not you who chose me, it was I who chose you"?

PRAYER

"Almighty and ever-living God, our source of power and inspiration, give us strength and joy in serving you as followers of Christ, who lives and reigns with you and the Holy Spirit, one God, forever and ever. Amen."
— Liturgy of the Hours
Saturday 29th Week of Ordinary Time

32

Desert Experience

"Jesus summoned the Twelve and began to send them out two by two, giving them authority over unclean spirits. He instructed them to take nothing on the journey but a walking stick — no food, no traveling bag, not a coin in the purses in their belts. They were, however, to wear sandals. 'Do not bring a second tunic,' he said, and added: 'Whatever house you find yourself in, stay there until you leave the locality. If any place will not receive you or hear you, shake its dust from your feet in testimony against them as you leave.' With that they went off, preaching the need of repentance. They expelled many demons, anointed the sick with oil, and worked many cures."

"The apostles returned to Jesus and reported to him all that they had done and what they had taught. He said to them, 'Come by yourselves to an out-of-the-way place and rest a little.' People were coming and going in great numbers, making it impossible for them to so much as eat. So Jesus and the apostles went off in the boat by themselves to a deserted place" *(Mark 6:7-13, 30-32).*

Jesus sent his disciples out with power to heal and to bring the Good News to many. When the disciples returned they were all excited about what they had accomplished. It was then that Jesus invited them: "Come by yourselves to an out-of-the-way place and rest a little."

Jesus wanted the disciples to rest and relax so that they could reflect on how powerfully God had worked through them. He wanted them to realize that it was not through their own efforts that they were able to accomplish so much, but through God's special gift to them. He wanted them to integrate into their lives this awareness of God's abiding presence and power operative within them. In this way they could be molded and transformed into effective disciples totally dependent on the Lord.

Jesus calls us to active ministry in the world. He knows that our busyness can subtly sidetrack us away from him. He knows, furthermore, that when we become too involved in the secular demands, we will eventually become secularized, frustrated, disappointed, burned out.

Jesus invites us to a desert experience regularly. We need to ponder what God is doing in our lives and what he is asking of us. He encourages us to come aside to be alone with him, to reflect on what God has wrought through us.

Jesus invites us to "come by yourselves to an out-of-the-way place" to rest with him and reassess his goodness in giving us life, in energizing us at every moment of the day, in providing for all our needs.

Jesus wants to bring us to a deeper appreciation that he is our Savior and Redeemer, eager and anxious to forgive and heal us if we will only come to him with humble and contrite hearts.

Jesus asks us to believe in his love for us. He wants us to realize that he loves us just as we are. He doesn't care what we might have done or not done in the past, he still loves us.

Jesus wants us to relax in his presence, to let him love us, to be alone with him regularly and consistently. He says: "Be still and know that I am God."

Jesus wants us to relish our privacy with him and to permit nothing to rob us of our daily date with him in prayer. During this time he urges us to let go of all the plans, programs and projects in which we are involved and to be exclusively for him as he is for us.

As we ponder these wishes of Jesus, we must face ourselves honestly and objectively. The Lord will ask nothing from us except what is for our benefit. Jesus himself took time out frequently in his busy ministry to be alone with his Father. He knows how much we need to do the same. Our unwillingness to do so could be a rejection of his invitation which we can ill afford. He awaits our decision!

REVIEW OF LIFE

Do I give the Lord the time he deserves and the time I need to live a happy and peaceful existence on this earth?

Do I frequently appraise my pursuits in life to ascertain whether or not they are the Lord's will or my own ambitions?

Do I face myself honestly about the use of my time, trying to discover if I am entering into a deeper, richer relationship with the Lord?

Do I set aside time to make a retreat alone with the Lord, or some kind of a desert experience?

COLLOQUY

Jesus, during your brief sojourn on earth, you were frequently "absorbed in prayer," "spending the whole night in communion with God." By your example you teach me how necessary it is for me to make time for prayer. Grant me the grace and generosity to visit with you each day with a listening heart. Amen.

33

Special Ministry

"On one occasion Jesus spoke thus: 'Father, Lord of heaven and earth, to you I offer praise; for what you have hidden from the learned and the clever you have revealed to the merest children. Father, it is true. You have graciously willed it so. Everything has been given over to me by my Father. No one knows the Son but the Father, and no one knows the Father but the Son — and anyone to whom the Son wishes to reveal him. Come to me, all you who are weary and find life burdensome, and I will refresh you. Take my yoke upon your shoulders and learn from me, for I am gentle and humble of heart. Your souls will find rest, for my yoke is easy and my burden light' " *(Matthew 11:25-30)*.

We are living in the computer age of highly technical knowledge. We pride ourselves on our ability to accomplish unheard-of phenomena.

We risk becoming a proud, self-sufficient people. Our technological prowess can lead us away from God. Our sophisticated knowledge and technology can wean us away from our sense of dependence upon God.

In this spirit of self-sufficiency and independence, we can question the divine moral code such as the sacredness of life, the fulfillment of our natural desires. We can reject the teachings of the Church, because we do not understand the Church as the mystery of God's kingdom among us.

All this can bring disastrous results. We live in fear of annihilation in a nuclear holocaust. We experience the breakdown of human rights. We are bordering on zero population control.

All this can rob us of fulfillment. As a result we are living in an age of escapism: be it over-extended activity, pleasure madness, chemical dependency, even suicide.

Fulfillment and happiness are sought in these areas where they cannot be found. No escape can satisfy the hunger of the human heart for that peace and joy which has God as its source.

Fear and frustration, worry and anxiety, sometimes bordering on despair, characterize our times. In the midst of all of this comes an invitation from "the gentle and humble heart" of Jesus:

> "Come to me, all you who are weary and find life burdensome, and I will refresh you."

Jesus has called each one of us to a special ministry. No one else can ever do what the Lord has asked us to do. No one can love him for us. No one can serve him in the same capacity to which he has called us.

The Father has gifted and graced each one of us with special personal traits, with certain gifts and talents, which will aid us in fulfilling our ministry. In using our giftedness as God intended, we find happiness and peace.

In his loving concern for us, Jesus does not expect us to accomplish our task alone. He is there to assist us. In fact, he cautioned us: "Apart from me, you can do nothing" (John 15:5). This is just another way of saying: "With me, you can do all things." For this reason, Jesus bids us:

> "Take my yoke upon your shoulders and learn from me. . . . Your souls will find rest, for my yoke is easy and my burden light."

A yoke is usually a wooden bar or frame by means of which draft animals, such as oxen, are joined together to pull a load. It is a kind of harness which enables a team to pull together.

Mark Jesus' words. He did not promise to come to help us to pull our yoke. On the contrary, Jesus bids us to take his yoke upon us. He is pulling the load and merely asking us to help him.

In the Holy Land I saw a good illustration of what Jesus was trying to say. An Arab farmer was plowing on one of the many terraces with an old-fashioned plow. He had hitched a camel and a donkey together as a team. The huge camel was plodding along taking long strides and pulling most of, if not all, the load. The little donkey was taking quick choppy steps striving desperately to keep abreast of the big camel. He was not even able to keep the traces taut.

This is what Jesus does for us. He is pulling most of the load. He is asking only our willingness to help. He is asking only for our acceptance of any yoke which might come our way.

This invitation from Jesus should cause us to pause and reassess our attitudes toward the eventualities which come our way.

Our willingness, or our refusal, that is the question!

REVIEW OF LIFE

Do I love enough to accept gladly whatever the Lord sends my way?

Do I recognize my total dependency on the Lord, aware that without him I can do nothing?

In trouble and difficulty do I first turn to the Lord, or do I usually seek advice and help elsewhere?

When I have successfully accomplished something, do I thank the Lord?

COLLOQUY

Jesus, what a generous promise you made that if I come to you when life becomes burdensome, you would always be there to refresh me and help to carry my load. Unfortunately, too often, I turn first to others for help and encouragement. Only when all else fails do I turn to you. Teach me that wisdom which will bring me first, last and always to you.

34

As I Have Done

"Do you understand what I just did for you? You address me as 'Teacher' and 'Lord,' and fittingly enough, for that is what I am. But if I washed your feet — I who am Teacher and Lord — then you must wash each other's feet. What I just did was to give you an example: as I have done, so you must do. I solemnly assure you, no slave is greater than his master; no messenger outranks the one who sent him. Once you know all these things, blest will you be if you put them into practice" (John 13:12-17).

Our purpose in life is to become more and more Christlike. That's what it means to be a Christian. We are to "put on the new man" as St. Paul urges us. We are to reflect the image of Jesus and radiate his goodness as we strive to pattern our own life after his example.

We must ask ourselves, how would Jesus act or react in these circumstances? Then we need to survey our own attitudes and actions to discover whether or not they reflect the heart of Jesus.

Jesus manifested his great love for us by his humble, loving service. It was his boundless love for us which prompted him to say of himself:

"Such is the case with the Son of Man who has come, not to be served by others, but to serve, to give his own life as a ransom for the many" *(Matthew 20:28)*.

Service is an expression of love for others. Jesus demonstrated his unconditional love throughout his entire ministry, but especially in the upper room when he washed the feet of his apostles.

In Jesus' day the common footwear was sandals. With dusty roads in the dry season and muddy paths in the rainy season, it was customary to wash the feet of the guests as they arrived before entering a house. As a rule this task was performed by a menial. However, if the host wanted to show special deference to a visitor, he would perform this service himself.

None of the disciples of Jesus would acknowledge himself as the lowest among them. On the contrary, they were striving to sit on his right and on his left in the kingdom. For this reason Jesus himself washed the feet of the disciples to give them a memorable example.

Jesus did so to prepare them for the Eucharist and to give them a sense of belonging to him and to each other — a sense of family, of community. Jesus performed this service appealing to us to express our love of neighbor in such a concrete way.

> "Do you understand what I just did for you? You address me as 'Teacher' and 'Lord,' and fittingly enough, for that is what I am. But if I washed your feet — I who am Teacher and Lord — then you must wash each other's feet. What I just did was to give you an example: as I have done, so you must do."

Jesus may not ask us literally to wash the feet of another, but he does want us to offer our loving service in whatever capacity the occasion requires. We have the opportunity to manifest our love for others in hundreds of different ways throughout the course of each day.

In his missive to Timothy, St. Paul outlined some

criteria that should characterize the deportment of widows, which, of course, is standard conduct for all Christians. Here are a few of the norms which St. Paul enumerates:

"Her good character will be attested to by her good deeds. Has she brought up children? Has she been hospitable to strangers? Has she washed the feet of Christian visitors? Has she given help to those in distress? In a word, has she been eager to do every possible good work? (I Timothy 5:10).

As we ponder Paul's checklist we could enlarge on it endlessly. No doubt occasions such as the following present themselves daily:

- refraining from speaking about myself;
- a visit or phone call to a shut-in;
- a note of appreciation for some person's kindness to ourselves or to others;
- a congratulatory message to one who has accomplished an unusual task;
- a sympathetic concern for a person who has lost a loved one, or met with some tragedy;
- a radiant smile even for a stranger;
- a friendly rather than a formal greeting.

As we add to this enumeration, can we not hear Jesus say: "As I have done, so must you do"?

REVIEW OF LIFE

Am I willing to abandon my own plans such as giving up a restful, relaxing evening when another person needs me?

Do I consider certain tasks and duties beneath my dignity, or too trivial for my time and attention?

Am I a good listener when someone needs to talk or do I

become impatient and restless when listening to them?

Do I convey the impression that I am very busy when someone needs my help?

COLLOQUY

Lord, Jesus, how compelling is your example as you washed the feet of your disciples! How convincing are your words: "as I have done, so you must do," yet how consistently I lack the generosity and graciousness to be available to others. Help me to overcome my self-centeredness by performing an act of loving service to the very first person I meet today.

Finale

35

Prince of Peace

" 'Peace' is my farewell to you, my peace is my gift to you; I do not give it to you as the world gives peace. Do not be distressed or fearful. You have heard me say, 'I go away for a while, and I come back to you.' If you truly loved me you would rejoice to have me go to the Father" *(John 14:27-28)*.

When Isaiah foretold the coming of the Messiah, he used a number of titles which would describe the mission of the Redeemer who was to come into the world. One of the titles he used to describe the work of the Messiah was "Prince of Peace" *(Isaiah 9:5)*. Jesus came into the world as the Prince of Peace and by his redemptive suffering certainly earned that title.

Jesus began his immediate redemptive work with his triumphal entry into Jerusalem. It is significant that Jesus rode into the Holy City mounted on a donkey. The donkey was a symbol of peace while a horse symbolized war. Jesus' passion and death was to bring God's peace to the hearts of all persons; hence the appropriateness of his entry on a donkey.

After his resurrection Jesus frequently used the greeting: "Peace be with you" *(John 20:19)*. He repeated this greeting again and again to impress upon us that he redeemed our fallen nature and restored our relationship with the Father once again. One of the many fruits of his redeeming love is a genuine and profound peace.

Jesus was certainly aware that the peace which he won for all mankind would seem rather general and universal to us. For this reason he instituted the Sacrament of Penance in which we encounter him personally and privately so that we ourselves experience that peace which comes to us with the realization that we are forgiven.

This awareness of being forgiven personally is the source of great peace and consolation for each one of us. As we experience his mercy and compassion, we will certainly enjoy that peace which the world cannot give. Peace is always a sure criterion of living in God's favor.

Peace is a dynamic establishing a threefold relationship. Peace is, likewise, the fruit of this genuine triple relationship. When we are at peace with God, at peace with our neighbor, at peace with ourselves, then we will know that joy and tranquility, that comfort and contentment, which is the fruit of the Spirit. In the Our Father, we pray that we will be able to recognize more fully God as our loving Father, our brothers and sisters as the children of our common Father and ourselves as the adopted sons and daughters of our Father. When this relationship comes into proper perspective in our lives then we will enjoy genuine peace.

Reconciliation is the indispensable avenue to attain this goal. Our brokenness and woundedness requires reconciliation and healing in many areas of our life. Genuine peace is the fruit of humble, sincere reconciliation.

St. Paul bids us rejoice in the peace which Jesus gained for us:

"God's own peace, which is beyond all understanding, will stand guard over your hearts and minds, in Christ Jesus" (Philippians 4:7).

Speaking of those "under the domination of sin" and unwilling to turn contritely to the Lord, Paul says:

"The path of peace is unknown to them; the fear of God is not before their eyes" (Romans 3:17-18).

The prophet also prepared us for the peace which would be ours when the Lord forgives us.

"Thus is my bitterness transformed into peace. You have preserved my life from the pit of destruction, when you cast behind your back all my sins" (Isaiah 38:17).

Our compassionate Father respects the free will with which he endowed us. He does not force us to accept forgiveness, nor does he force us to receive the Sacrament of pardon and peace, but he eagerly awaits our coming to him.

Jesus may have reason to weep for us as he did over the city of Jerusalem.

"Coming within sight of the city, he [Jesus] wept over it and said: 'If only you had known the path to peace this day; but you have completely lost it from view! . . . you failed to recognize the time of your visitation' " (Luke 19:41ff).

Hopefully we are not failing to recognize God's loving mercy and compassion channeled to us through this Rite of Reconciliation.

Jesus graciously gifts us with his peace:

" 'Peace' is my farewell to you, my peace is my gift to you" (John 14:27).

REVIEW OF LIFE

Does Jesus weep because of my neglect to meet him in this Sacrament of pardon and peace?

When I am troubled or disturbed, or when my heart is heavy, do I seek healing by encountering Jesus in the Sacrament of Penance?

Do I really appreciate how eager Jesus is to share his grace by removing any barrier which may be deflecting his peace from me?

In my prayer, do I listen with all my heart as Jesus says: "Peace be with you"?

PRAYER

"Lord, may the saving sacrifice of your Son, our King and peacemaker, which we offer through these sacramental signs of unity and peace bring harmony and concord to all your children. We ask this through Christ our Lord. Amen."

— Sacramentary — Mass for Peace

"May he grant you joy of heart and may peace abide among you; May his goodness toward us endure . . . as long as the heavens are above" (Sirach 50:23-24).

OTHER POPULAR BOOKS
by Msgr. David E. Rosage

QUANTITY

_____ Discovering Pathways to Prayer — 3.95

_____ Encountering the Lord in Daily Life — 4.50

_____ Linger With Me — 3.95

_____ Praying With Mary — 3.50

_____ Praying With Scripture in the Holy Land — 3.95

Available at your bookstore or from
LIVING FLAME PRESS
Box 74, Locust Valley, N.Y. 11560

NAME_____

ADDRESS _____

CITY_____ STATE _____ ZIP_____

Payment enclosed. Kindly include $.70 postage and handling on orders up to $5; $1.00 on orders up to $10; more than $10 but less than $50 add 10% of total; over $50 add 8% of total. Canadian residents add 20% exchange rate, plus postage and handling.